The Madinan Way

The Soundness of the Basic Premises
of the School of the People of Madina

by
Ibn Taymiyya

Bookwork

© 1420/ 2000 Bookwork

Published by:
  Bookwork
  6 Terrace Walk
  Norwich NR1 3JD
  ABewley@compuserve.com
  http://www.angelfire.com/ab2/bookwork

Production: Bookwork, Norwich

Translation: Aisha Bewley
Editor: Abdalhaqq Bewley
http://ourworld.compuserve.com/homepages/ABewley
http://bewley.virtualave.net
Cover design: Aarlsen, Norwich

ISBN 0 9538639-0-5

Distributed by Ta-Ha Publishers
1 Wynne Road
London SW9 0BB U.K.
website: http://www.taha.co.uk
e-mail: sales@taha.co.uk

Printed at:
Biddles Limited
Guildford, Surrey

Table of Contents

The Text of the Question
which Ibn Taymiyya was asked

The Shaykh of Islam, Ibn Taymiyya, may Allah have mercy on him, was asked about the soundness of the basic premises of the school of the people of Madina, the position of Malik to whom their school in the Imamate and the *deen* is ascribed, and his precision in the sciences of the *Shari‘a* in the opinion of the scholars of all the cities of the Muslims and the people of reliability and experience of all ages.

His reply was as follows:

Praise belongs to Allah. It is the school of the people of the City of the Prophet, the Abode of the *Sunna*, the Abode of the *Hijra*, and the Abode of Victory. It was in Madina that Allah fashioned the *Sunna* and the *Shari‘a* of Islam for His Messenger Muhammad, may Allah bless him and grant him peace. It was to Madina that the *Muhajirun* emigrated to Allah and His Messenger, and it was in Madina that the Ansar were located (*"Those who were already settled in the abode and in belief"* (59:9)). In the time of the Companions, the Followers and their Followers, their school was the soundest of the schools of the people in all the cities of Islam, east and west, both in respect of its fundamental principles and its secondary rulings.

The excellence of Madina and its people according to Hadith

These three periods – those of the Companions, the Followers and their Followers – comprise the period of the most excellent generations whom the Prophet, may Allah bless him and grant him peace, mentioned in a hadith which is sound in every respect:

> "The best of generations is the generation among whom I was sent, and then those who follow them and then those who follow them."

Ibn Hibban mentioned the two generations after his generation which are undisputed. In certain hadiths there is some uncertainty about the third generation after the Prophet's generation. It is definitely stated in some of them that the third generation after his generation is confirmed, and thus there are four generations mentioned in total.

Ibn Hibban al-Busti and hadith scholars like him throughout the generations of this community have authoritatively stated that to be true. So this additional generation is confirmed in the *Sahih* Collections.

As regards the hadith about the three generations, we read in the two *Sahih* collections that 'Abdullah ibn Mas'ud reported that the Messenger of Allah, may Allah bless him and grant him peace, said, "The best of my community is the generation who follow me and then those who follow them and then those who follow them. Then there will come a people who will be such that the testimony of one of them will precede his oath and his oath will precede his testimony." In the *Sahih* of Muslim, 'A'isha, may Allah be pleased with her, said, "A man asked the Messenger of Allah, may Allah bless him and grant him peace, 'Which people are the best?' He said, 'The generation among whom I was sent, and then the second, and then the third.'"

As for the uncertainty regarding the fourth generation, we find in the two *Sahih* collections that 'Imran ibn Husayn reports that the Messenger of Allah, may Allah bless him and grant him peace, said, "The best of you is my generation and then those who follow them and then those who follow them." 'Imran said, "I do not know whether the Messenger of Allah, may Allah bless him and grant him peace, said it two or three times after his generation." He then said, "Then after them there will come a people who testify when they are not asked to testify, who betray and are not trustworthy, and who make vows and do not keep them. Plumpness will appear among them." One version has: "The best of this community is the generation among whom I was sent, and then those who follow them and then those who follow them." He is also reported as stating in the hadith, "They swear when they are not asked to swear."

In the *Sahih* of Muslim, Abu Hurayra said, "The Messenger of Allah, may Allah bless him and grant him peace, said, 'The best of my community are those among whom I was sent, and then those who follow them.' Allah knows best whether he mentioned the third or not. 'Then will come a people who love plumpness. They will testify before they are asked to testify.'"

His words in these hadiths "they will testify before they are asked to testify" have been understood by a group of scholars to mean testifying to the truth before being asked for it by the person on whose behalf the testimony is made. They apply that to something about which the witness has knowledge, joining this to the words of the Prophet, "Shall I inform you of the best of witnesses? The one who brings his testimony before he is asked for it." They say that the second refers to a situation where the evidence to which he is asked to testify is produced and he acknowledges it.

The sound position is that the censure in these hadiths is regarding those who bear false witness, as has come in various texts of the hadith: "then lying spreads among them to such an extent that a man will testify when he is not asked to testify." This is why it is connected to treachery and failing to fulfil vows. These three qualities are the signs of a hypocrite, as is confirmed in the agreed-upon hadith in which the Prophet, may Allah bless him and grant him peace, said, "There are three signs of a hypocrite: when he speaks, he lies; when he makes a promise, he breaks it; and when he is trusted, he betrays his trust." The text of Muslim has, "even if he fasts and prays and claims that he is a Muslim." So the Prophet censured them for the qualities of hypocrisy which were going to spread among them. He made it clear that they would rush to lie, to the point that a man would testify to a lie even before he was asked to do so and therefore be worse than someone who does not lie until he is asked to lie.

As far as the fourth generation is concerned, it is similar to what we find in the two *Sahih* collections from Abu Sa'id al-Khudri. The Prophet, may Allah bless him and grant him peace, stated, "A time will come upon people when groups of people go out to raid and will be asked, 'Are there among you any who saw the Messenger of Allah, may Allah bless him and grant him peace?' and they will say, 'Yes,' and will be given victory. Then groups of people will go out to raid and will be asked, 'Are there among you any who saw the Companions of the Messenger of Allah, may Allah bless him and grant him peace?' and they will say, 'Yes,' and will be given victory. Then groups of people will go out to raid and will be asked, 'Are there among you any who saw the companions of the Companions of the Messenger of Allah, may Allah bless him and grant him peace?' and they will say, 'Yes,' and will be given victory. Then groups of people will go out to raid and will be asked, 'Are there among you any who saw the companions of the companions of the Companions of the Messenger of Allah, may Allah bless him and grant him peace?' and they will say, 'Yes,' and will be given victory." The text of al-Bukhari has, "Then a time will come upon people when groups of people go out to raid." That is what he said in the second and third, and in all of them he said, "kept the company" and did not say "saw".

Muslim has in another variant: "A time will come upon people when missions will be sent from among them and they will say, 'See if you find any of the Companions of the Messenger of Allah, may Allah bless him and grant him peace,' and a man will be found and they will be given victory on his account. Then a second mission will be sent and they will say, 'Are there any among you who saw the Companions of the Messenger of Allah, may Allah bless him and grant him peace?' and they will say, 'Yes,' and they will be given victory. Then a third mission will be sent and they will say, 'See if you can find among you anyone who saw someone who saw the Companions of the Messenger of Allah, may Allah bless him and grant him peace.' Then the fourth mission will take place and it will be said, 'See if you can find among you anyone who saw anyone who saw anyone who saw the Companions of the Messenger of Allah, may Allah bless him and grant him peace.' and a man will be found and they will be given victory on his account."

The hadith of Abu Sa'id indicates two things. It indicates that a Companion of the Messenger of Allah, may Allah bless him and grant him peace, is anyone who saw him and believed in him, even if this was only for a short time, as Imam Ahmad ibn Hanbal and other Imams have stated. Malik said, "Anyone who kept the company of the Messenger of Allah, may Allah bless him and grant him peace, for a year, a month, or a day, or just saw him, and believed in him, is one of his Companions. He has his status of Companionship accordingly. The expression "Companionship" is generic and contains different categories. One says that his Companionship was for a month or an hour." So it is clear in this hadith that the principle of Companionship is connected to those who saw him and believed in him. That must be the case.

In Muslim's second path of transmission, four generations are mentioned. Those who affirm this additional generation say that this is reliable and the fact that the other hadiths do not mention it does not negate its existence. Similarly, there is uncertainty in the hadith of Abu Hurayra about whether the third generation is mentioned, but this does not detract from the rest of the sound hadiths which affirm the third generation. Those who do not acknowledge it say that in the sound hadith of Ibn Mas'ud he reported that after the three generations there will come a people whose testimony precedes their oath and whose oath precedes their testimony. So there is censure mentioned after the third generation. It can also be said that there is in fact no contradiction between the two reports. Lying may well appear in the fourth generation and yet, in spite of this, there could be someone on whose account victory would be given because of the connection of direct vision.

The consensus of the people of Madina is considered to be evidence, as opposed to other Muslim cities

During the time of those generations which the Messenger of Allah, may Allah bless him and grant him peace, praised, the school of the people of Madina was the soundest of the schools of the people of all the Muslim cities. The people of Madina confined themselves to following in the footsteps of the Messenger of Allah, may Allah bless him and grant him peace, more than the people of any other city. In addition to this, the people of other cities had less knowledge of the Prophetic *Sunna* and followed it less completely. Thus the people of Madina were not in need of any sort of administration from rulers above them. The needs of other scholars and the requisites of those who worship was greater than the need of the people of Madina since the Madinans were richer than other people in all these matters because of the extensive living record of the Prophet which they possessed and about which everyone needs knowledge and must follow.

This is why none of the Muslim scholars believed that the consensus of any of the cities except Madina was a proof which must be followed – not in those times nor after them; not the consensus of the people of Makka or Syria or Iraq or any other of the cities of the Muslims. Anyone who relates from Abu Hanifa or any of his companions that the consensus of the people of Kufa is a proof which every Muslim must follow, has, by that statement, accused Abu Hanifa and his companions of going astray. As far as Madina is concerned, people have discussed the consensus of its people and it is well-known from Malik and his companions that the consensus of its people is a proof, even if the rest of the Imams vie with them about that.

The discussion is confined to their consensus during that first excellent period. After that period, everyone agrees that the consensus of its people is no longer a proof since at that time there were great scholars elsewhere who were not in Madina, especially after the Rafidites[1] made their appearance there. The people of Madina continued to adhere to their ancient school, ascribing themselves to the school of Malik, up until the beginning of 600 AH or thereabouts, when some of the Rafidites of the east from the people of Qashan and others of the most corrupt schools arrived there and became numerous, especially those who designated themselves members of the family of the Prophet. Books of the people of innovation which are not in harmony with the Book and *Sunna* reached them and provided them with many erroneous ideas and, for that reason, innovation has been frequent there from that time on.

---

1. The Rafidites were one of the major Islamic sects. Their name derives from the fact that Zayd ibn 'Ali ibn al-Husayn ibn 'Ali refused to curse Abu Bakr and 'Umar. He said, "They were the wazirs of my ancestor, Muhammad," and so they rejected (*rafada*) his opinion. It is said that it is because they rejected the opinion of the Companions because they had offered allegiance to Abu Bakr and 'Umar. They were the ones who maintained that 'Ali should have been khalif after the Messenger.

Innovations, like the Shi'a and the Qadariyya, issued from almost all cities except Madina

During the time of the three excellent generations, there was no evident innovation in Madina at all and no innovation issued from it at all regarding the basic premises of the *deen*, such as emerged from all the other cities. The major places in which the Companions of the Messenger of Allah, may Allah bless him and grant him peace, lived and from which knowledge and belief spread out were five: Makka and Madina, Iraq and further east, and Syria. From them went forth the Qur'an, hadith, *fiqh*, and worship and all matters of Islam which are followed.

Fundamental innovations emerged from all these cities except the city of the Prophet. From Kufa emerged the Shi'a and Murji'ites, who later spread elsewhere. From Basra emerged the Qadariyya, the Mu'tazilites and other unsound religious practices which later spread elsewhere. Syria had the Nasibiyya and the Qadariyya. The Jahmiyya emerged from a region of Khorasan, and this is the worst innovation of them all.

The appearance of innovations was in proportion to the distance of their place of origin from the Abode of the Prophet. When the split occurred after the murder of 'Uthman the innovation of the Haruriyya [Kharijites] made its appearance. As regards their punishment, they fall into three categories: the extremists whom 'Ali burned with fire, the *Mufaddala*, on whom he imposed eighty lashes, and the Saba'ites whom he threatened. He intended to punish Ibn Saba' by death or some other punishment, but he escaped from him.

Then during the final days of the period of the Companions, the Qadariyya arose at the end of the lifetime of Ibn 'Umar, Ibn 'Abbas, Jabir and their like among the Companions. The Murji'ites also came into existence at about that time.

As for the Jahmiyya, they originated at the end of the time of the Followers, after the death of 'Umar ibn 'Abdu'l-'Aziz. It is related that he had warned against them. The Jahmites appeared in Khorasan during the khalifate of Hisham ibn 'Abdu'l-Malik. The Muslims had executed their Shaykh, al-Ja'd ibn Dirham, some time before that. Khalid ibn 'Abdullah al-Qasri executed him. He said, "O people! Sacrifice and Allah will accept your sacrifices. I am slaughtering al-Ja'd ibn Dirham who claimed that Allah did not take Ibrahim as a friend and did not speak directly to Musa. Very high exalted is Allah above what al-Ja'd ibn Dirham says!" Then he got down and slaughtered him. It is related that that reached al-Hasan al-Basri and his like among the Followers, and they were thankful for it.

The city of the Prophet, however, did not generate any of these innovations. Even if there might have been a few people there who concealed their adherence to one or another of these sects, the Madinans' opinion of them was that they were all contemptible and blameworthy. There were people of the Qadariyya and others there, but they were censured and overcome, which was not the case with the Shi'a and Murji'ites in Kufa, and the Mu'tazilites and other innovations in Basra, and the Nasibiyya in Syria. There they were blatant.

It is established in the *Sahih* Collections that the Prophet, may Allah bless him and grant him peace, stated that the Dajjal will not enter Madina. There is a famous story in which 'Amr ibn 'Ubayd, the leader of the Mu'tazilites, passed by someone who was conversing with Sufyan ath-Thawri but he did not know that he was Sufyan. 'Amr asked that man, "Who is this?" He replied, "This is Sufyan," or he said, "One of the people of Kufa." He said, "If only I had known that, I would have invited him to accept my opinion, but I thought that he was one of those Madinans who are unassailable."

Knowledge and belief remained manifest there until the time of Malik's followers. They are the people of the fourth generation, since that generation took from Malik and the people of his generation, like ath-Thawri, al-Awza'i, al-Layth ibn Sa'd, Hammad ibn Zayd, Hammad ibn Salama, Sufyan ibn 'Uyayna and their likes. These men took from the groups of the Followers who in turn took from those who had met the Companions.

The four levels of the consensus of the people of Madina

The discussion about the consensus of the people of Madina in that period and the resolution of the "question of the consensus of the people of Madina" includes looking at those things on which all the Muslims agree and those which represent the position of the majority of the Imams of the Muslims and those which are only upheld by a few of them. In other words the consensus of the people of Madina falls into four categories.

The first is that which proceeds by direct transmission from the Prophet, may Allah bless him and grant him peace, like their transmission of the amount of the *sa'* and the *mudd* measures, and like not having to pay *zakat* on vegetables, and the *habous* or *waqf*. This is something that constitutes a proof by the agreement of all the scholars. Ash-Shafi'i, Ahmad ibn Hanbal, and their companions consider it to be an undisputed proof, just as Malik considers it to be a proof. And that is also the school of Abu Hanifa and his people.

When Abu Yusuf, may Allah have mercy on him, the most important of the people of Abu Hanifa and the first to be accorded the title "Qadi of the Qadis", met with Malik and asked him about these questions, Malik replied to him with the multiple (*mutawâtir*) transmission of the people of Madina. Abu Yusuf reverted to Malik's statement and said, "If my companion [i.e. Abu Hanifa] had seen the same as I have seen, he would have reverted as I have reverted."

Abu Yusuf thus asserted that such transmission constitutes a proof in the eyes of his companion, Abu Hanifa, just as it is a proof in everyone else's eyes. However this transmission simply did not reach Abu Hanifa just as many hadiths did not reach him nor did they reach other Imams. They cannot be blamed for leaving something, knowledge of which did not reach them. Abu Yusuf's reverting to this form of transmission is the same as his reverting to many hadiths which he and his companion Muhammad [ash-Shaybani] followed, which meant abandoning something their shaykh [Abu Hanifa] had said, since they knew that their shaykh used to say, "These hadiths are also a proof if they are sound." However those hadiths did not reach him.

Whoever thinks that Abu Hanifa and other Imams of the Muslims deliberately opposed sound hadiths by analogy or anything else, has erred about them and is either speaking by supposition or by caprice. This man, Abu Hanifa, followed the *hadith* about doing *wudu'* with *nabidh* on a journey, something which is contrary to analogy, and the hadith about laughing in the prayer[1] which is also contrary to analogy since he was confident that they were sound, even if Imams of hadith do not consider them sound.

We made this clear in our treatise, *The Removal of Censure from Notable Imams,* and we made it clear that none of the Imams of Islam opposed a sound hadith without a valid reason. Indeed, they had about twenty reasons. For instance, the hadith did not reach one of them, or it reached him in a manner which was not reliable, or he did not believe that it indicated a ruling, or he believed that that indication was contradicted by something stronger than it, like its being abrogated or something that indicates abrogation and other similar things. The excuse is that regarding some things the scholar is correct, and so he has two rewards, and regarding some things he makes a mistake after striving to reach the truth, and so he is rewarded for his striving and his mistake is forgiven by the words of Allah Almighty, *"Our Lord, do not take us to task if we forget or make a mistake!"* (2:283) It is confirmed in the *Sahih* that Allah answers this supplication and says, "I have done it." It is also because the scholars are "the heirs of the Prophets," as is reported in a sound hadith by at-Tirmidhi.

---

1. Abu Hanifa held that laughing in the prayer also breaks *wudu'*.

Allah mentioned that Da'ud and Sulayman gave judgement in a case and that He made one of them understand it and did not censure the other one. Rather He praised both of them since He gave each of them judgement and knowledge: *"And Da'ud and Sulayman when they gave judgement about the field when the people's sheep strayed into it at night. We were witnesses to their judgement. We gave Sulayman understanding of it. We gave each of them judgement and knowledge."* (21:78-79)

This judgement contains two points about which scholars disagree: the question of animals wandering into fields at night, for which the owner is liable according to the majority of scholars like Malik, ash-Shafi'i and Ibn Hanbal, although Abu Hanifa does not make him liable. The second question is whether liability is on the basis of like for like or on the basis of equivalence of value. There is disagreement about that in the school of ash-Shafi'i and Ibn Hanbal and others.

What is related from the majority of the *Salaf* in such cases is that liability on the basis of like for like is demanded if the person is capable of fulfiling it, just as Sulayman judged. Most *fuqaha'* only make that liability on the basis of equivalence of value, as is known in the school of Abu Hanifa, ash-Shafi'i and Ahmad ibn Hanbal.

What is meant by all this is that the transmission of the practice (*'amal*) of the people of Madina is treated as a proof by the agreement of the Muslims, as Malik told Abu Yusuf when he asked him about the *sa'* and the *mudd*. He ordered the people of Madina to bring their *sa'* measures and they told him how they had been handed down to them from their ancestors. He asked, "Do you think, Abu Yusuf, that these people are lying?" He replied, "No, by Allah, they are not lying." He said, "I measured these *sa's* and I found them to be five and a third *ritls*, according to your *ritls*, people of Iraq." He said, "I will revert to your statement, Abu 'Abdullah. If my companion [Abu Hanifa] had seen the same as I have seen, he would have reverted as I have reverted."

Then he asked him about the *zakat* on vegetables, and he said, "The people of Madina did not collect *zakat* on them in the time of the Messenger of Allah, may Allah bless him and grant him peace, nor did Abu Bakr, nor 'Umar, may Allah be pleased with both of them." He meant the vegetables which were grown there.

He asked him about the *habous* and he said, "This is the *habous* of so-and-so and this is the *habous* of so-and-so," mentioning them to make it clear that they were Companions. Abu Yusuf said about each question, "I have reverted, Abu 'Abdullah. If my companion had seen the same as I have seen, he would have reverted as I have reverted."

Abu Yusuf and Muhammad ibn Hasan agree with the rest of the *fuqaha'* about there being no *zakat* on vegetables, as is the school of Malik, ash-Shafi'i, and Ibn Hanbal, and about there not being any *zakat* on less than five *wasqs*, as is the school of those men, and that the *waqf* is binding, as is the school of those men.

Malik said, "Your *ritls*, people of Iraq," because when the Umayyad dynasty came to an end and the dynasty of the descendants of al-'Abbas arrived shortly afterwards, the Abbasid Abu Ja'far, entitled al-Mansur, built Baghdad and made it the capital of his kingdom. Abu Ja'far (al-Mansur) knew that at that time the people of the Hijaz were more concerned with the *deen* of Islam than the people of Iraq and it is related that he mentioned that to Malik or another of the scholars of Madina. He said, "I have looked into this business and I found the people of Iraq to be a people of lies and fraud," or words to that effect, "and I found the people of Syria to be people of raiding and *jihad*, and I found this business with you." It is reported that he said to Malik words to the effect, "You are the most knowledgeable of the people of the Hijaz."

Abu Ja'far asked the scholars of the Hijaz to move to Iraq and to disseminate knowledge there. Hisham ibn 'Urwa, Muhammad ibn Ishaq, Yahya ibn Sa'id al-Ansari, Rabi'a ibn Abi 'Abdu'r-Rahman, Hanzala ibn Abi Sufyan al-Jumahi, 'Abdu'l-'Aziz ibn Abi Salama al-Majishun and others went there. Abu Yusuf used to frequent the assemblies of these men and learned hadiths and more from those who came from the Hijaz. This is why it is said about the companions of Abu Hanifa that Abu Yusuf was the one among them with the most knowledge of hadith, Zufar was the one to most avoid analogy, al-Hasan ibn Ziyad al-Lu'lu'i was the greatest of them in knowledge of secondary rulings, and Muhammad [ash-Shaybani] had the most knowledge of them of Arabic and reckoning, and perhaps it is said that he was the greatest of them in knowledge of secondary rulings. When Iraq became the capital of the *Umma* and it was needed to teach its people the *Sunna* and the *Shari'a*, the legal measure was changed to the *ritl* of the people of Iraq. Their *ritl* was based on heavy wheat and lentils when that is 90 *mithqals*: 128 dirhams and 4/7 dirham.

This is the first degree of the consensus of the people of Madina, and it is considered a proof by the agreement of all the Muslims.

The second degree is the early practice in Madina before the murder of 'Uthman ibn 'Affan. It is considered to be a proof in the school of Malik and it is so stipulated by ash-Shafi'i. He is quoted by Yunus ibn 'Abdu'l-A'la as saying, "When you see that the early ones of the people of Madina did something, then do not let any doubt that it is the truth arise in your heart." The same applies to the clear school of Ahmad ibn Hanbal – the usual practice of Rightly-guided Khalifs is a proof which must be followed. Ahmad ibn Hanbal said, "Every oath of allegiance given in Madina was part of the khalifate of Prophethood." It is known that the oath of allegiance to Abu Bakr, 'Umar, and 'Uthman took place in Madina. Similarly the oath of allegiance to 'Ali took place in Madina, and then he left it, and after that there was no other oath of allegiance given in Madina.

There is the hadith reported by al-'Irbad ibn Sariya from the Prophet, may Allah bless him and grant him peace, which is confirmed as a sound hadith. It is: "You must follow my *Sunna* and the *sunna* of the guided, Rightly-guided khalifs after me. Cling to it and hold fast to it with your teeth! Beware of innovated matters! Every innovation is misguidance."

The *Sunan* collections of Abu Dawud and at-Tirmidhi contain the hadith reported by Safina from the Prophet, may Allah bless him and grant him peace: "The khalifate of Prophethood will last thirty years, and then it will become a harsh kingdom."

It is related that Abu Hanifa deemed the statement of the Rightly-guided Khalifs to be a proof and no early practice of the people of Madina in the time of Rightly-guided Khalifs was known to be contrary to the *Sunna* of the Messenger, may Allah bless him and grant him peace.

The third degree is when there are two contrary indications regarding a question, like two hadiths or two analogies, and it is not known which is the more correct, and one of them was acted upon by the people of Madina. There is disagreement about this. The school of Malik and ash-Shafi'i is that one prefers the practice of the people of Madina, and the school of Abu Hanifa is that one does not prefer the practice of the people of Madina.

The people of Ahmad ibn Hanbal have two approaches here. One, which is the position of Qadi Abu Ya'la and Ibn 'Aqil, is that the practice of the people of Madina does not predominate. The second, which is the position of Abu'l-Khattab and others, is that it does predominate. It is said that this is quoted from Ibn Hanbal and that part of what he said is, "When the people of Madina see a hadith and act by it, it is the limit."

He used to give *fatwa* based on the school of the people of Madina and put it ahead of the school of the people of Iraq with great determination. He used to direct people who asked for *fatwa* to the schools of the people of hadith and the school of the people of Madina, and he would direct people who asked for *fatwa* to Ishaq, Abu 'Ubyad, Abu Thawr, and their likes among the *fuqaha'* of the people of hadith, and he would direct them to the circle of the Madinans, the circle of Abu Mus'ab az-Zuhri and his like.

Abu Mus'ab was the last of those who transmitted the *Muwatta'* from Malik to die. He died a year after Ibn Hanbal in 242 AH. Ibn Hanbal used to dislike the people of Madina being rebutted in the way that the people of opinion were rebutted. He would say, "They follow the living tradition (*athâr*)."

These are the schools of the majority of the Imams which agree with the school of Malik in giving predominance to the positions of the people of Madina.

The fourth degree is the later practice in Madina. Is this a proof in the *Shari'a* which must be followed or not? The Imams of the people say that it is not a proof in the *Shari'a*. This is the school of ash-Shafi'i, Ahmad ibn Hanbal and Abu Hanifa and others. It is also the position of established Maliki scholars, as the excellent 'Abdu'l-Wahhab mentioned in his book, *The Bases of Fiqh*. He stated that this is neither consensus nor a proof in the view of established Maliki scholars, while it might be considered a proof by some of the people of the Maghrib among Malik's followers. The Imams have neither text nor indication of it. Rather they are people of imitation (*taqlid*).

I said: I have not seen anything that Malik said which obliges this to be made a proof. We find in the *Muwatta'* that he mentioned the proof on which they agree. He reports their school. Sometimes he says, "That which the people of knowledge still do in our land," which refer to an earlier consensus. Sometimes he does not say that.

If Malik had believed that the later practice was a proof which the entire community is obliged to follow, even if it differs from the texts, he would have been obliged to make people hold to that as much as possible, just as he had to oblige them to follow the hadith and firm *sunna* about which there is no contradiction, and that is by consensus. Harun ar-Rashid or someone else offered to compel people to adopt the *Muwatta'*, but Malik rejected that saying, "The Companions of the Messenger of Allah, may Allah bless him and grant him peace, dispersed into different cities. I have only gathered the knowledge of the people of my city," or words to that effect.

Just as it is clear that the consensus of the people of Madina differs from the schools of the majority of the Imams, it is also known that their position is the soundest of the positions of the people of all the cities in respect of both transmission and opinion. Sometimes it constitutes a decisive proof, sometimes a strong proof, and sometimes it is just probable by the indication that none of the other cities of the Muslims possesses any of this special characteristic.

It is known that those of the Companions who were in Madina were the best of the Companions since no one left it before the *Fitna* without someone better than him remaining there. When Syria and Iraq and other places were conquered, 'Umar ibn al-Khattab, may Allah be pleased with him, sent people to the cities to teach them the Book and the *Sunna*. 'Abdullah ibn Mas'ud, Hudhayfa ibn al-Yaman, 'Ammar ibn Yasir, 'Imran ibn Husayn, Salman al-Farisi and others went to Iraq. Mu'adh ibn Jabal, 'Ubada ibn as-Samit, Abu'd-Darda', Bilal ibn Rabah and their likes went to Syria. There remained with him men like 'Uthman, 'Ali, and 'Abdu'r-Rahman, and those like Ubayy ibn Ka'b, Muhammad ibn Maslama, Zayd ibn Thabit, and others.

Ibn Mas'ud was the most knowledgeable of the Companions in Iraq at the time when the *Fitna* took place. Then he came to Madina and questioned the men of knowledge of the people of Madina and they made him retract some things he had said and return to their practice, as occurred regarding the question of wives' mothers when Ibn Mas'ud thought that the precondition referred to them and to stepdaughters, and that when a man divorced his wife before consummation, her mother was lawful for him just as her daughter had been lawful. When he came to Madina and asked about that, the men of knowledge of the Companions informed him that the precondition referred to the stepdaughters rather than the mothers and so he returned to their position and commanded the man to separate from his wife after she was pregnant.

The practice of the people of Madina was either a *sunna* from the Messenger of Allah, may Allah bless him and grant him peace, himself or they referred to the judgements of 'Umar ibn al-Khattab. It is said that Malik took the bulk of the *Muwatta'* from Rabi'a, and Rabi'a from Sa'id ibn al-Musayyab, and Sa'id ibn al-Musayyab from 'Umar, and 'Umar is truthful. At-Tirmidhi related that the Messenger of Allah, may Allah bless him and grant him peace, said, "If I had not been sent among you, then 'Umar would have been sent among you." In the two *Sahih* Collections, the Prophet said, "In the nations before you there were men who were inspired. If there is such a one among my community, it is 'Umar." In the *Sunan*, the Prophet said, "Follow those who come after me: Abu Bakr and 'Umar."

'Umar used to consult the great Companions, like 'Uthman, 'Ali, Talha, az-Zubayr, Sa'd, and 'Abdu'r-Rahman. They were the people of consultation (*shura*). This is why ash-Sha'bi said, "Examine the judgements that 'Umar made. He used to consult people." It is known that that on which 'Umar gave judgement or *fatwa*, and on which he consulted them, carries more weight than the judgement or *fatwa* of Ibn Mas'ud or his like, may Allah be pleased with all of them.

In questions of the *deen*, both in respect of the roots and the branches, 'Umar used to follow the judgement of the Messenger of Allah, may Allah bless him and grant him peace, and he used to consult 'Ali and others of the people of consultation, just as he consulted with him about a woman observing the *'idda* (waiting-period) of a reversible divorce when her husband had a fatal illness about whether she inherited, and similar things.

When 'Uthman was murdered and the *Fitna* and division occurred, and 'Ali moved to Iraq, as did Talha and az-Zubayr, no one like those men remained in Madina. However, still there were Companions like Sa'd ibn Abi Waqqas, Abu Ayyub,

Muhammad ibn Maslama and their likes who were more important than the Companions who were with 'Ali.

So know that among the Companions who were in Kufa were 'Ali and Ibn Mas'ud and that 'Ali had been in Madina when 'Umar, 'Uthman and Ibn Mas'ud were there. He was the representative of 'Umar and 'Uthman. It is known that 'Ali had more knowledge and excellence than that of all of the people of Iraq who were with him. That is why ash-Shafi'i used to argue with some of the people of Iraq about *fiqh*, using the statement of 'Ali and Ibn Mas'ud as an argument against his opponent. Ash-Shafi'i wrote *The Book of the Disagreement of 'Ali and 'Abdullah (ibn Mas'ud)* clarifying in it what his opponent and others of the people of knowledge had abandoned of what the two of them had said. Muhammad ibn Nasr al-Marwazi came after him and wrote even more on that than ash-Shafi'i had written. He said, "You and the rest of the Muslims abandon what the two of them said for something that is preferred to what they said. It is like that when other people abandon that for what is preferred to it."

Part of what will clarify that is that all the Muslim cities except for Kufa followed the knowledge of the people of Madina. They did not consider themselves to be equal to them in knowledge – like the people of Syria and Egypt, like al-Awza'i and those Syrians before and after him, and like al-Layth and those before and after him of the Egyptians. Their esteem for the practice of the people of Madina and the fact that they followed them in their early schools is clear and evident. The same applies to the scholars of Basra, like Ayyub, Hammad ibn Zayd, 'Abdu'r-Rahman ibn Mahdi, and their likes.

This is why the school of the people of Madina prevailed in those cities. The people of Egypt became supporters of the position of the people of Madina and Egypt was the home of many important Malikis, like Ibn Wahb, Ibn al-Qasim, Ashhab, and 'Abdullah ibn 'Abdu'l-Hakam, and the Syrians like al-Walid ibn Muslim, Marwan ibn Muhammad and their likes. They have well-known transmissions from Malik.

As for the people of Iraq like 'Abdu'r-Rahman ibn Mahdi and Hammad ibn Zayd, and like Qadi Isma'il ibn Ishaq and their like, they followed the school of Malik, and they were head *qadis*. Isma'il and his like were among the most important scholars in Islam.

As for the Kufans after the *Fitna*, they claimed to be equal to the people of Madina. Before the *Fitna*, they followed the people of Madina and imitated them. Before the murder of 'Uthman, it is not known that any of the people of Kufa or anyone else claimed that the people of their city knew more than the people of Madina. When 'Uthman was murdered and the Community divided and split into parties, then there appeared among the people of Kufa those who claimed that the scholars of the people of Kufa were equal to the scholars of the people of Madina.

✻ ✻ ✻ ✻ ✻

One aspect of the uncertainty regarding this is that the position of Madina was weakened when it ceased to be the seat of the khalifate and the position of the people of Iraq was strengthened when it moved there. Discussion of the questions of the branches and fundamental principles was, however, already established during 'Umar's khalifate. It is well-known that the position of the people of Kufa with respect to the rest of the cities before the split was more correct than their statements and hadiths after the split. 'Abida as-Sulmani, the Qadi of 'Ali, may Allah be pleased with him, said, "We prefer your opinion which coincided with that of 'Umar to your opinion after the split which was yours alone."

The sectarianism and divisiveness of Kufa is well-known, as is indicated by both text and consensus, since the Prophet, may Allah bless him and grant him peace, stated, "The *fitna* (civil strife) will come from over there. The *fitna* will come from over there. The *fitna* will come from over there where the horn of Shaytan rises." (i.e. in the east). This hadith is confirmed in the *Sahih* Collections without any detraction.

Part of what will clarify this matter is that knowledge is either by transmission or opinion (*ra'y*).

The people of Madina were the soundest of the people of the cities in both transmission and opinion. Their hadiths are the soundest of hadiths. The people of knowledge of hadith agree that the soundest of hadiths are the hadiths of the people of Madina and then the hadiths of the people of Basra. As for the hadiths of the people of Syria, they are less sound than those. They do not have the connected *isnads* and precision of expression that those others possess.

Among the people of Madina, Makka, Basra and Syria at that time, there was not anyone who was known for lying, but there were some who were precise and some who were not precise.

As for the people of Kufa, there were no people of any city who lied more than they did. In the time of the Followers, there were many people who were known for lying, especially the Shi'a. The various sects there were the parties most frequently given to lying by the agreement of the people of knowledge. It is for this reason that it is mentioned from Malik and others of the people of Madina that they did not accept as evidence the general hadiths of the people of Iraq because there were known to be liars among them, and the Iraqis could not distinguish between those who were truthful and the liars. When they knew that a hadith was true, then they would use it as a proof. For instance, Malik related from Ayyub as-Sakhtiyani, who was an Iraqi. He was asked about that and he said, "I have not related from anyone without Ayyub being better than him."

This position is the early position of ash-Shafi'i so that it is related that he was asked about an instance when Sufyan related a hadith from Mansur from 'Alqama from 'Abdullah which he did not use as evidence. He said, "It has no root in the Hijaz. Otherwise I would use it." Then ash-Shafi'i retracted that and told Ahmad ibn Hanbal, "You know more hadiths than we do. When a hadith is sound, inform me about it so that I can believe it, no matter whether it is Syrian, Basran or Kufan." He did not say Makkan or Madinan because he was already using them as a proof.

As for the scholars of the people of hadith like Shu'ba, Yahya ibn Sa'id and the authors of the *Sahih* and the *Sunan* collections, they used to distinguish between the people of reliable memory and others. So in Kufa they knew who were the reliable people concerning whom there was no doubt and among them there were people who were better than many of the people of the Hijaz. No scholar would suspect such companions of 'Abdullah ibn Mas'ud as 'Alqama, al-Aswad, 'Abida as-Sulmani, al-Harith at-Taymi and Shurayh the Qadi. Then those like Ibrahim an-Nakha'i and al-Hakam ibn 'Utayba and their like were among the most reliable of people and those with the soundest memories.

This is why the scholars of Islam agree about using as evidence those whom the people of knowledge of hadith have declared sound, whatever city they may be from. Abu Dawud as-Sijistani wrote *Individuals of the People of the Cities* in which he mentioned those whom the people of every Muslim city had singled out as being people of knowledge of the *Sunna*.

As for the people of *fiqh* and opinion (*ra'y*), it is known that the people of Madina did not have anyone among them who originated an innovation in the basic premises of the *deen*. When there was discussion about opinion at the beginning of the Abbasid dynasty and Rabi'a ibn Hurmuz divided up the branches for them, as 'Uthman al-Busti and his likes had done in Basra and Abu Hanifa and his likes in Kufa, there came to be people who accepted that and people who rejected it.

Those who rejected it were such men as Hisham ibn 'Urwa, Abu'z-Zinad, az-Zuhri, Ibn 'Uyayna and their likes. If they rejected an opinion which originated in Madina, the opinion which originated in Iraq was even more strongly rejected. The people of Madina did not exceed the people of Iraq in what is not praised, but they were over them in what is praised, and it is by that that predominance occurs.

Hisham ibn 'Urwa said, "The tribe of Israel remained just until the half-breeds spread among them: the sons of the captives of other nations. Then they spoke among them by opinion, and they were excessive and led others astray." Ibn 'Uyayna said, "We investigated that and we found that judgements based on opinion originated among the part-Arabs, the sons of the captives of other nations. He mentioned some of those who were in Madina, Basra and Kufa, and those in Madina were more praiseworthy than those who were in Iraq of the people of Madina.

When Malik, may Allah be pleased with him, said that one of the two dynasties [Umayyads and Abbasids] followed the *sunan* more than the other dynasty, he said that because of the innovations that appeared in connection with it because those others were more entitled to the khalifate by lineage and proximity.

Al-Mansur, al-Mahdi and Harun ar-Rashid, who were the foremost of the Abbasid khalifs, preferred the scholars of the Hijaz and their position over the scholars of the people of Iraq, just as the Umayyad khalifs had preferred the people of Hijaz over the people of Syria. Then there arose among them those who did not follow this course, and instead inclined to the greatly fabricated opinions of the east and thus the khalifate was weakened.

Then Baghdad began to be the home of true knowledge and belief and it predominated over other cities after the death of Malik and his like among the scholars of the Hijaz. There were then people living in Baghdad who spread the *Sunna* there and who expounded the realities of Islam, such as Ahmad ibn Hanbal and Abu 'Ubayd and those like them among the *fuqaha'* of the people of hadith.

In that time the *Sunna* appeared there in both its basic premises and branches, and there was much of it there, and from there it spread to the other cities, and from that time it also spread in the east and west. In the east there were men like Ishaq ibn Ibrahim ibn Rahawayh and his companions, and the companions of 'Abdullah ibn al-Mubarak. And some of the knowledge of the people of Madina which had been transmitted to them from the scholars of hadith went to the west. There was then knowledge in Baghdad, Khorasan and the Maghrib the like of which was not to be found at that time in Madina and Basra.

As for the situation of the Hijaz, after the time of Malik and his companions there were from that time no scholars of the Hijaz who were better than the scholars of the east, Iraq and the Maghrib.

This subject is too large to pursue. If we were to deal in full with the excellence of the scholars of the people of Madina and the soundness of their basic premises, the discussion would be very lengthy indeed.

※ ※ ※ ※ ※

The position of Malik in respect of transmission and opinion

It is absolutely clear, and no one has any doubt, that Malik, may Allah be pleased with him, was the strongest of the people of the school of the people of Madina in respect of both transmission and opinion. There was no one in his time or after him who was stronger in those things than him. His position among the people of Islam, both the elite and the common, is not hidden from anyone who has the least whiff of knowledge.

Abu Bakr al-Khatib has compiled the reports of those who transmitted from Malik and they reached about 1700. They are only those whose hadiths reached al-Khatib after about 300 years, so how about those whose reports were cut off or whose reports did not reach him? Al-Khatib died in 462 AH and he was contemporary with Ibn 'Abdu'l-Barr, al-Bayhaqi, Qadi Abu Ya'la and others like that, while Malik died in 179 AH and Abu Hanifa died in 150 AH and ash-Shafi'i died in 204 AH and Ahmad ibn Hanbal died in 241 AH.

Ash-Shafi'i, may Allah be pleased with him, said: "There is no book under heaven more correct after the Book of Allah than the *Muwatta'* of Malik," and it is just as ash-Shafi'i said. This is not a contradiction of what the Imams of the Muslims said about there not being after the Qur'an any book sounder than the *Sahih* Collections of al-Bukhari and Muslim, the Imams agreeing that al-Bukhari is sounder than Muslim. Whoever prefers Muslim, prefers it because he compiles together all the versions of each hadith in the same place. That is easier for someone who wants to collect all the versions of the hadith.

As for people who claim that the hadiths which are in Muslim alone, or the men which he alone takes from, are sounder than the hadiths which are in al-Bukhari alone or the men which he alone takes from, this is an error about which no scholar has any doubt, just as no one has any doubt that al-Bukhari had more knowledge of the hadith, their faults, and history than Muslim, and that he knew more *fiqh* than him. Al-Bukhari and Abu Dawud knew the most *fiqh* of any of the people of the *Sahihs* and famous *Sunan*. If it does happens that something found in Muslim alone is preferred to something in al-Bukhari alone, this is a rare occurrence; the reverse is usually the case. That on which the people of knowledge agree is that after the Qur'an there is no book sounder than the books of al-Bukhari and Muslim.

These two books enjoy this position because they are devoted to the hadiths with a sound *isnad*. Their aim in compiling these collections was not to mention the traditions of the Companions and the Followers nor even all of the hadiths which are good and the *mursal* hadiths and the like of that. There is no doubt that a book devoted to hadiths with sound *isnads* from the Messenger of Allah, may Allah bless him and grant him peace, must be the soundest of books because it represents the soundest transmission in any written book from the one who was protected from all falsehood.

As for the *Muwatta'* and books like it, they were written in the manner of the scholars who wrote at that time. In the time of the Messenger of Allah, may Allah bless him and grant him peace, people used to write down the Qur'an. The Prophet, may Allah bless him and grant him peace, had forbidden them to write down anything other than the Qur'an from him. He said, "Anyone who has written down anything except the Qur'an should efface it." Then that was abrogated, according to the majority of the scholars, when writing was permitted for 'Abdullah ibn 'Amr. He said, "Dictate something for my father." He wrote a document for 'Amr ibn Hazm. They said that the initial prohibition was out of fear of making the Qur'an like something else. Then when there was no danger of that, permission was granted. From that time on people used to write down what they wrote of the hadiths of the Messenger of Allah, may Allah bless him and grant him peace, and they also wrote down other things.

They did not organise that in book form until the time of the Followers of the Followers. Then knowledge was written down, and the first to write something about *tafsir* and something about the dead was Ibn Jurayj. Sa'id ibn Abi 'Uruba, Hammad ibn Salama, Ma'mar and such men wrote on the subject of the Prophet, the Companions and the Followers. These are the books of *fiqh*, knowledge, roots and branches after the Qur'an. Malik wrote the *Muwatta'* in this manner. He wrote after 'Abdullah ibn al-Mubarak, 'Abdullah ibn Wahb, Waki' ibn al-Jarrah, 'Abdu'r-Rahman ibn Mahdi, 'Abdu'r-Razzaq, Sa'id ibn Mansur and others.

These are the books which were under consideration in that time which ash-Shafi'i indicated when he stated, "There is no book after the Qur'an more correct than the *Muwatta'* of Malik. His hadiths are sounder than the hadiths of his peers."

It was the same when Imam Ahmad was asked about the hadiths and opinions of Malik and the hadiths and opinions of others. He preferred the hadiths and opinions of Malik over the hadiths and opinions of those people.

This confirms the hadith which at-Tirmidhi and others related from the Prophet, may Allah bless him and grant him peace,

"A time is soon coming when people will beat their camels in search of knowledge and will not find a man of knowledge with more knowledge than the man of knowledge of Madina." It is related from more than one, and Ibn Jurayj, Ibn 'Uyayna and others stated that it refers to Malik.

Those who disagree about this have two outlets. One is to attack the hadiths, some of them claiming that they are curtailed and incomplete, and the other is to say that it is someone other than Malik who is meant, and that it should be someone like al-'Umari az-Zahid (meaning al-Qasim ibn Muhammad).

It is said that what this hadith indicates, and the fact that it is Malik who was meant, is a confirmed matter for all who were present then, and by multiple transmission (*tawâtur*) for all who were not there. There is no doubt that there was no one in the time of Malik to whom people drove their camels more than Malik. This is confirmed in two respects.

The first is by seeking his precedence over the likes of ath-Thawri, al-Awza'i, al-Layth, and Abu Hanifa. There is disagreement about this, and there is no need to discuss it in this context.

The second is that it is said that Malik died after all these men. He died in 179 AH and all of them died before that. So it is known that after the death of those men, there was no one in the Community at that time with more knowledge than Malik. None of the Muslims disputes this, and no one travelled to any of the men of knowledge of Madina as they travelled to Malik, neither before nor after him. People travelled to him from the east and the west, and people of different generations travelled to him. Among them were scholars, ascetics, kings and common people. His *Muwatta'* spread throughout the land until there was no book after the Qur'an at that time known to have a greater dissemination than the *Muwatta'*.

The people of the Hijaz, Syria and Iraq took the *Muwatta'* from him. Some of the youngest to take it from him were ash-Shafi'i, Muhammad ibn al-Hasan ash-Shaybani and their likes. In Iraq, when Muhammad ibn al-Hasan transmitted knowledge from Malik and the Hijaz, his house was full, but when he transmitted from the people of Iraq few people came since they knew that the knowledge of Malik and the people of Madina was sounder and firmer.

The two people from whom ash-Shafi'i took the bulk of his knowledge were Malik and Ibn 'Uyayna. It is known by everyone that Malik was more important than Ibn 'Uyayna so that he used to say, "Malik and I are as the speaker says:

'When the three-year old camel colt is short in the horn,
    it cannot attack the powerful nine year old.'"

As for those who claim that the one to whom the camels were beaten in search of knowledge was al-'Umari az-Zahid[1], although he was an ascetic righteous man who commanded the right and forbade the wrong, it is not known that people had need of any of his knowledge or travelled to him for it. When he wanted to ascertain something he would consult Malik and ask for his decision about it, as it is transmitted that he consulted him when he wrote to him from Iraq about them taking on the khalifate there. He said, "Not until I consult Malik." When he consulted him, he indicated that he should not involve himself in the matter and informed him that the descendants of al-'Abbas would not give it up without a lot of blood being spilled over it. He mentioned to him what 'Umar ibn 'Abdu'l-'Aziz had mentioned when he was told, "Appoint al-Qasim ibn Muhammad." He said, "The Umayyad family will not give up this command until a lot of blood is spilled over it."

It is not known that people took any knowledge of *tafsir*, hadith, *fatwas* or other things from al-'Umari az-Zahid, so how can he be compared to Malik in respect of knowledge and the people travelling to him for it?

Then, even in the books of *Sahih* Collections, of which the book of al-Bukhari is the most important, the first hadith with

---

1. Meaning al-Qasim ibn Muhammad ibn Abi Bakr.

28

which he begins the chapter is the hadith of Malik, and if there is any hadith of Malik on a subject, he does not put other hadiths ahead of it. We know that people beat their camels to Madina in search of knowledge and did not find any man of knowledge with more knowledge than Malik in his time.

With regard to Malik and the people of Madina, all other people are either in agreement or in dispute. Anyone who agrees with them is a helper and supporter, and anyone who disputes with them still respects them and esteems them, acknowledging their worth. You will not find anyone who disparages their words and school except for someone who is not considered to be one of the leaders of knowledge. That is because they know that Malik is the mainstay of the school of the people of Madina.

It is evident to both the elite and common people that the school of the people of Madina predominates over those of other cities. The *Muwatta'* is filled either with the hadiths of the people of Madina or with things on which the people of Madina agreed, old or new. As for those questions about which the people of Madina and others differed, he chose a position concerning them and said, "This is the best of what I have heard," thus following the traditions accepted by the men of knowledge of Madina.

We do not deny that there are some people who deny Malik, first using their hadiths as a means of disputing some questions, as is mentioned from 'Abdu'l-'Aziz ad-Darawardi. He was asked about the question of the amount of the bride-price being determined by the minimum for theft. He was told, "Acknowledge the truth, 'Abdullah!" i.e. you have taken the position of the people of Iraq who determine the minimum of the bride-price as the minimum amount of theft, but the minimum with Abu Hanifa and his companions is ten dirhams, and with Malik, ash-Shafi'i, and Ibn Hanbal, the minimum is three dirhams or four dinars, as has come in sound hadiths.

It is said first of all that such stories indicate the weakness of the position of the people of Iraq in the sight of the people of

Madina, and that they used to dislike people agreeing with them [the Iraqis]. This is famous among them – that they would fault a man for that, as Ibn 'Umar said when he was asked for a *fatwa* about the blood of gnats.[1] It is the same as Sa'id ibn al-Musayyab's words to Rabi'a when he asked him about the blood-wit for a woman's fingers.

Secondly, such a statement is very rare indeed in the words of Malik. There is no scholar who does not have something which can be refuted. How excellent is what Ibn Khuwayzimandad said about the question of selling and renting books of opinion *(ra'y)*. "We believe that there is no difference between the opinion of our master Malik and others in this ruling, but he was less subject to error than other people."

The majority of the hadiths which we find from Malik come through one of two main transmissions, even though some of them were abandoned by his companions, such as the question of lifting the hands when going into *ruku'* and when coming up from it.

The people of Madina related from Malik that the hands should be raised in accordance with the sound hadith which he related, but Ibn al-Qasim and other Basrans took an earlier trans-mission. It is known that the reason for the writing of the *Mudawwana* of Ibn al-Qasim was the *Questions* of Asad ibn al-Furat which he derived from the people of Iraq. Then Asad asked Ibn al-Qasim about them and he replied to him either with a direct transmission from Malik or sometimes with an analogy based on his words. Then its means of transmission was Sahnun. This is why the words of Ibn al-Qasim contain a bias towards the words of the people of Iraq, even if that is not one of the bases of the people of Madina.

---

1. He replied with disdain that they were worried about the blood of gnats but not worried about spilling the blood of the grandson of the Prophet at Karbala'.

30

The reason for the spread of the school of Malik in Andalusia

It is agreed that the school of Malik spread in Andalusia. Yahya ibn Yahya was governor of Andalusia and the deputies consulted him and they used to order the *qadis* to judge first by his transmission from Malik and only then from the transmission of someone else.

So the transmission of Ibn al-Qasim from Malik spread because it was acted on and it was predominant in the school of the practice of the people of Madina and the *Sunna*, to such an extent that they began to abandon the transmission of the *Muwatta'* which was passed on by multiple transmissions from Malik. Adter his death they continued to relate it only by the transmission of Ibn al-Qasim, even though a group of Maliki Imams objected to that. If there is any fault in such a thing, it must be held against the transmitter of it, not against Malik himself. All who follow his school will follow the *Sunna* in matters in general since there is little of the *Sunna* regarding which there is not a statement on which that school agrees, as opposed to most of the school of the people of Kufa. They often go contrary to the *Sunna*, even if that is not their intention.

Then whoever reflects on the basic premises of Islam and the pillars of the *Shari'a* will find that the basic principles of Malik and the people of Madina are the soundest of basic premises and rules. Ash-Shafi'i, Ibn Hanbal and others confirmed that. When ash-Shafi'i argued with Muhammad ibn al-Hasan ash-Shaybani when Muhammad preferred his companion [i.e. Abu Hanifa} over the companion of ash-Shafi'i [i.e. Malik], ash-Shafi'i said to him, "By justice or by pride?" He said, "By justice." He said, "I ask you by Allah, who has better knowledge of the Book of Allah, our companion or your companion?" He said, "Rather your companion has." He said, "Who has better knowledge of the *Sunna* of the Messenger of Allah, our companion or your companion?" He said, "Rather your companion has." He said, "Who has better knowledge of the statements of the Companions of the Messenger of Allah, our companion or your companion?" He said, "Rather your companion has." He said, "Only analogy remains between us and you, and we will speak of analogy, but the truth is that the man who has more knowledge of the basic principles will also make the sounder analogy."

They asked Imam Ahmad, "Who has the better knowledge of the *Sunna* of the Messenger of Allah, may Allah bless him and grant him peace, Malik or Sufyan?" He said, "Malik has." He was asked, "Who has better knowledge of the traditions of the Companions of the Messenger of Allah, Malik or Sufyan?" He said, "Malik has." He was asked, "Which one had greater asceticism, Malik or Sufyan?" He said, "This is yours."

It is known that Sufyan ath-Thawri was the most knowledgeable of his generation in hadith in addition to his precedence in respect of *fiqh* and asceticism. Those who deny the people of Iraq and others in respect of those opinions which originated in Kufa, do not extend that to Sufyan ath-Thawri. Indeed, in their opinion, Sufyan is the Imam of Iraq. Ibn Hanbal's preference for the school of Malik over the school of Sufyan is his preference for the school of Madina over the school of the people of Iraq. Ibn Hanbal considered Sufyan ath-Thawri the foremost of his entire generation, and he had tremendous esteem for him. He knew, however, that the school of the people of Madina and its men of knowledge was closer to the Book and the *Sunna* than the school of the people of Kufa and their men of knowledge.

Ahmad ibn Hanbal was just and had great knowledge of these matters. He gave everything with a due its proper due. This is why he loved ash-Shafi'i and praised him and made supplication for him and defended him when anyone attacked ash-Shafi'i or attributed innovation to him. He would mention his esteem for the *Sunna* and his following it and his knowledge of the bases of *fiqh*, like the abrogating and abrogated, the general and the detailed. It is established that he argued on behalf of the school of the people of hadith against those who opposed it by opinion and other things. Ash-Shafi'i used to say, "In Baghdad, they used to call me the defender of hadith."

Ash-Shafi'i was known for his efforts to follow the Book and *Sunna* and his earnest striving to refute those who opposed that. He followed the school of the people of the Hijaz. He had learned *fiqh* first by the method of the Makkans, the companions of Ibn Jurayj, like Muslim ibn Khalid az-Zanji and Sa'id ibn Salim al-Qaddah. Then he travelled to Malik and took the *Muwatta'* from him and completed his study of the basic premises of the people of Madina. They were more important in knowledge and *fiqh* and worth than the people of Makka from the time of the Prophet, may Allah bless him and grant him peace, until the time of Malik. Then the Inquisition (*Mihna*) took place during which he went to Iraq and met with Muhammad ibn al-Hasan ash-Shaybani and copied out his books and debated with him. He learned the fundamental principles of Abu Hanifa and his followers, and he took what hadiths he took from the people of Iraq, and then he returned to the Hijaz.

Then he went to Iraq a second time during which he wrote his early book known as *The Proof*. Ahmad ibn Hanbal joined him in Iraq and also met him in Makka. Ishaq ibn Rahawayh met him and they debated in the presence of Ahmad ibn Hanbal, may Allah be pleased with all of them. He did not meet Abu Yusuf, al-Awza'i or others. Whoever mentions that in the journey ascribed to him is a liar. There are lies forged against him in respect of that journey and also against Malik, Abu Yusuf, Muhammad and others among the people of knowledge which are not concealed from men of knowledge. It is the sort of lying to be found in such stories. Abu Yusuf and Muhammad did not try to harm ash-Shafi'i at all and what is mentioned as having happened with Malik did not occur in the falsification of that journey.

Then ash-Shafi'i went to Egypt and wrote his new book and in his speech and writing he was ascribed to the school of the people of Madina such as Malik. He used to say, "Some of our companions," meaning the people of Madina or some of the men of knowledge of Malik or Malik himself.

He said in the course of his writing, "Some of the easterners opposed us." Ash-Shafi'i was one of the companions of Malik and was known as one of his companions. He chose to live in Egypt at that time because they followed the school of the people of Madina and those Egyptians who had a similar position, such as al-Layth ibn Sa'd and his like. Some of the people of the west followed the school of those men and some of them followed the school of al-Awza'i and the people of Syria. The school of the people of Syria and Egypt are close, but the people of Madina are considered better by all.

Since ash-Shafi'i was a man who sought knowledge and saw proofs in sound hadiths and other things, he had to follow them, even if that was in opposition to the position of his Madinan companions. Therefore he undertook what his opinion demanded of him and he composed a dictation on the questions of Ibn al-Qasim and displayed some divergence from Malik in certain things. Ash-Shafi'i was good in what he did and undertook what he had to, even if there were objections to that by those who disliked him and insulted him, and the well-known Egyptian inquisition took place. May Allah forgive all the believers, men and women, the living and the dead of them.

Abu Yusuf and Muhammad ash-Shaybani were the followers of Abu Hanifa and they were particularly connected to him, as ash-Shafi'i was particularly connected to Malik, but their disagreement with Abu Hanifa is close to ash-Shafi'i's disagreement with Malik. All of that stems from following proofs and undertaking what that obliges.

Ash-Shafi'i confirmed the basic premises of his companions and the Book and the *Sunna* but he often followed hadiths he considered to be sound. This is why 'Abdullah ibn 'Abdu'l-Hakam used to say to his son Muhammad, "My son, cling to this man. He possesses proofs. As soon as you say, 'Ibn al-Qasim said,' you will be laughed at if you go outside Egypt." Muhammad said,

"When I went to Iraq, I sat in a circle which contained Ibn Abi Du'ad and I said, 'Ibn al-Qasim said.' He said, 'Who is Ibn al-Qasim?' I said, 'A man who gives *fatwas* which are accepted from Egypt to Morocco.'" I think that he said, "I said, 'May Allah have mercy on my father.'"

He meant by that: Seek the proof behind the statement of your companions and do not simply follow. Imitation is only accepted where the one imitated is esteemed, as opposed to the legal proof, which is accepted in every place. Allah obliges every striver to say that which he is obliged to say according to the knowledge which he has. Allah singled out this person for knowledge and understanding in a way that He did not single out that one. This is one of those singled out for increase of knowledge and understanding in one type of knowledge or an area of it or a question, and that one is singled out in respect of another type of knowledge.

* * * * *

However, all the schools of the city of the Prophet are preferred in general over the schools of other people of the east and the west. That is evident when we examine general principles.

One of them is the principle of the *halal* and the *haram* as it is connected to impure things in water. It is known that Allah says in His Book, *"My mercy extends to all things but I will prescribe it for those who are godfearing and pay* zakat, *and those who believe in Our Signs; those who follow the Messenger, the Unlettered Prophet, whom they find written down with them in the Torah and the Gospel, commanding them to do right and forbidding them to do wrong, making good things lawful for them and bad things unlawful for them, relieving them of their heavy loads and the chains which were around them."* (7:156-157) Allah Almighty made good things lawful for us and forbade us bad things. Bad things are of two types; that which is bad in itself through something inherent in it, like blood, carrion and pig meat, and that which is bad through acquisition, such as something which is taken unjustly or acquired by an unlawful kind of contract like usury and gambling.

As for the first type, everything it is unlawful to have direct contact with, like impure things, is also unlawful to eat, but not everything which is unlawful to eat is also unlawful to touch, like poison. Allah forbade us certain things in respect of food and drink and forbade us certain things in respect of dress.

It is known that the school of the people of Madina, in respect of drinks, is more rigorous than the school of the Kufans. The people of Madina and all other cities and the *fuqaha'* of hadith make every intoxicant unlawful. So every intoxicant is considered to be wine and is therefore unlawful. If a lot of it makes one intoxicated, then a little of it is unlawful. The people of Madina do not argue about that, neither their earlier nor their later people, no matter whether the drink is from dates, grains, honey, horses' milk or anything else.

The Kufans, however, only consider wine to be that which becomes fermented from pressed grapes. If it is cooked before it becomes strong so that two-thirds evaporates, then they consider it to be lawful. The *nabidh* of dates and raisins is unlawful for them when it intoxicates if it is fresh, but if it is cooked, the least amount of cooking makes it lawful, even if it still intoxicates!

However, where food is concerned, the people of Kufa are more rigorous than the people of Madina. They consider unlawful every wild beast with fangs and every bird with talons. They make meats unlawful to the point that they consider lizards and hyenas to be unlawful. Horse meat is unlawful in their opinion according to one statement.

Malik, on the other hand, makes absolutely unlawful what has come in the Qur'an, and animals with fangs are either made unlawful, but with a less stringent prohibition, or they are disliked in the well-known position. It is related from him the that animals with talons are disliked. He does not make any bird unlawful nor dislikes eating it. The prohibition contains different degrees of prohibition. Malik dislikes eating horses, but both permission and prohibition are related from him.

Whoever considers the sound hadiths about this subject will know that the people of Madina follow the *Sunna* more closely. The subject of drinks is confirmed from the Prophet, may Allah bless him and grant him peace, in the hadiths which are known, by the one who knows them, to be the most conclusive hadiths by multiple transmission. Indeed, also sound from him is the prohibition of *nabidh* made from two things mixed together and even the use of certain vessels. This is not concealed from any who know the *Sunna*. As for foods, even if it were to be said that Malik differs with sound hadiths with regard to the prohibition, there is dispute about it. The sound hadiths which he differs with, making lizards and others things unlawful, are counterbalanced by others which are equal to them or exceed them. Furthermore these hadiths are very rare in relation to the hadiths about drinks.

Moreover, regarding those things Malik has traditions from the *Salaf,* like Ibn 'Abbas, 'A'isha, 'Abdullah ibn 'Umar and others to go along with his interpretation of the literal meaning of the Qur'an. The allowance of drinks does not have any text or analogy to justify it. It is, on the contrary, a statement which is in opposition to both text and analogy.

Furthermore, making something in the category of wine unlawful is stronger than making unlawful unwholesome meats. Wine must be absolutely avoided and the *hadd* punishment is obligatory for someone who drinks it. It is not permitted to purchase it and Malik permits its actual destruction following what has come in the *Sunna* about that. He even forbade someone making it into vinegar. All of this comes from following the *Sunna* which is not the case with the statement of those who oppose it among the people of Kufa. The repeated prohibition of drinks by the Lawgiver (the Prophet) is stronger than his prohibition of foods. Any statement which is in harmony with the Lawgiver is sounder.

Something that will help to make this clear is that a group of the people of Madina made singing lawful so that that began to be reported about the people of Madina. 'Isa ibn Ishaq at-Tabba' said, "Malik was asked about what some of the people allowed with regard to singing and he said, 'We consider those who do it to be corrupt.'" It is known that this is the least of what someone who makes drinks lawful considers to be lawful, and there are no texts derived from the Prophet, may Allah bless him and grant him peace, which forbid singing while there is the repeated prohibition of drinks. So he knew that the people of Madina followed the *Sunna* more closely.

Then one of the greatest of questions is that of something *halal* being mixed with that which is in itself *haram*, such as unclean things being mixed with water and other liquids. The people of Kufa make *haram* any water or liquid at all into which any impurity falls, whether large or small in amount, and then they reckon the extent to which the impurity reaches and they determine it to be ten cubits square.

Then some of them say that when any impurity falls into a well it cannot be used for purification, but can be drunk. Their *fuqaha'* say that it must be scooped out, either the estimated number of bucket-fulls of it, or all of it because of their statement that all water and liquids are made impure by something impure falling into them.

The people of Madina held a different view on that. In their view, water is only made impure if it is altered, although they do have two statements about whether a small amount of water becomes impure by a small amount of impurity. The school of Ibn Hanbal is close to that as is that of ash-Shafi'i. But these two calculate the small amount as being less than the two small amounts of Malik.

Malik says something different about foods. Similarly, there is disagreement in the school of Ahmad ibn Hanbal about all liquids and it is known that this most resembles the Book and *Sunna*. The name "water" remains, and the name which made it permitted before the occurrence remains. The *Sunna* of the Messenger of Allah, may Allah bless him and grant him peace, indicated that the well of Buda'a[1] or any other well does not become impure, and that is only contradicted by a hadith which is not explicit in respect of this dispute. That is the hadith of the prohibition against urinating into standing water. The judgement is specific to urine. Some of them stipulate that he must actually urinate in it rather than the urine running into it. It can also be taken to refer to a small amount of water.

It is said that the prohibition against urine does not mean that the water becomes impure. Rather it is forbidden because it would lead to impurity if there was a lot of it. It is also the case that there is no disagreement among the Muslims that the prohibition against urinating in standing water is not general to all waters. For instance the water of the sea is excepted by both text and consensus. It is like that with great bodies of water which cannot be scooped out and one of whose sides cannot be moved by moving the other side. Urine does not make such amounts impure by agreement.

It is the same regarding used water becoming impure. The position of the people of Madina and those who agree with them is that its purity remains by sound hadiths from the Prophet, may Allah bless him and grant him peace, like the hadith of pouring his left-over *wudu'* water over Jabir, and his words, "The believer does not become impure," and other similar things.

That is also the case with their judgement about the lack of impurity of the urine of a child who has not yet eaten solid food. The school of some of the people of Madina and those who agree with them about this is supported by sound hadiths regarding it from the Prophet, may Allah bless him and grant him peace, which nothing else contradicts.

Thus the school of Malik and the people of Madina about impure things in respect of acts of worship has the closest possible resemblance to the sound hadiths and the conduct of the

---

1. Buda'a was the home of the Banu Sa'ida in Madina.

Companions. They did not say that the urine and faeces of animals whose meat can be eaten is impure. There are approximately ten proofs from texts and the ancient consensus and proper consideration to that effect. We have mentioned them on another occasion. Things have come to be considered impure by words which are supposed to be general while they are in fact not general, or by an analogy which makes the branch equal to root which is not the case.

Because of this, impurities are considered by the Maliki school to be unwholesome things and therefore unlawful in themselves and their position respecting that is taken from the position of the Kufans. This is also the case with foods: what those people consider impure is much more extensive. When it is said to the Madinans, "Your position contradicts the hadith about the licking of the dog and others like it concerning impurities," and also that it differs from the hadith about birds of prey and similar things, there is nonetheless no doubt that this involves less divergence from the texts than is the case with someone who considers as impure the urine and faeces of animals whose meat can be eaten, or some of them, or dislikes food left by cats.

Some people believe that all faeces and urine are pure except for human urine and faeces. The proof given in support of this position is no more unlikely than that of the people of Kufa, and those who agree with them, who consider as impurities what the people of Madina do not consider to be so.

If anyone contemplates the school of the people of Madina and knows the *Sunna* of the Messenger of Allah, may Allah bless him and grant him peace, it will be absolutely clear to him that the school of the people of Madina, which is constituted to make things in this domain easy, more closely resembles the *Sunna* of the Messenger of Allah, may Allah bless him and grant him peace, than a position which is so constituted as to make things difficult. The Prophet said in the sound hadith when the bedouin urinated in the mosque after he ordered that water be poured on his urine, "You have been sent to make things easy.

You have not been sent to make things difficult." This is the school of the people of Madina and the people of hadith. Those who oppose them say: "It must be washed and it is not permitted just to pour water." A *mursal* hadith which is not sound is related about that.

Section: Things being unlawful on account of their manner of acquisition

As for the second category of unlawful things, things which it is unlawful to acquire, like property which is taken unjustly by all types of usurpation such as theft, treachery and force, and like money which is obtained by means of usury and gambling, and like something which is taken in exchange for an unlawful item or service, like money gained from the sale of wine, blood, pigs, idols, prostitution, consulting a soothsayer and things like that, the position of the people of Madina in respect of that is the justest of all positions.

The prohibition of injustice and anything which brings about injustice is much stronger than the prohibition of the first category. Allah forbade bad things in food since they give unwholesome nourishment which in turn brings about injustice in man. So when someone is nourished by pigs and blood and beasts of prey, he begins to resemble what he is nourished by and so injustice and wrong flow into him commensurate with his nourishment.

Such food is allowed in the case of someone who is forced to consume it because the benefit of survival takes precedence over avoiding this evil. However, that is something which is incidental and has no harmful effect on him when a strong need exists. As for injustice, both a little and a lot of it is unlawful, and the Almighty made it unlawful for Himself and He made it unlawful for His slaves.

He made usury unlawful because it involves injustice. It is to take an increase without giving any equivalent for it. The prohibition of usury is stronger than the prohibition of gambling, which is wagering, because the usurer receives a precise increase from someone in need, and the gambler may obtain increase or may not. He wagers this against that, and he may win or lose.

The Prophet, may Allah bless him and grant him peace, forbade sales in which there is an element of uncertainty, *mulamasa* and *munabadha* sales,[1] selling fruits before their soundness is clear, and the *habal al-habala*,[2] and other such things which involve a kind of gambling. There is leeway in this in the case of someone who is compelled to it by a pressing need and enters into it following someone else, as there is an allowance for selling fruits after their soundness has appeared but before their soundness is complete, even though some parts of them may not become fully formed. There is also an allowance to buy palm trees which have been pollinated, along with their new fruits, if the buyer stipulates that even though their soundness has not yet appeared. This is permitted by the consensus of the Muslims, and that is the case with the rest of the trees which have fruits which have appeared. The seller is entitled to the fruits of pollinated date palms when the buyer did not stipulate them and so the tree belongs to the buyer but the seller benefits by it since that fruit remains on it until the time of cutting.

It is confirmed in the *Sahih* Collections that Malik commanded that a reduction should be made for disease in the fruit and said, "If you sell fruit to your brother and then disease afflicts it, it is not lawful for you to take any of the money of your brother. By what right will you take the money of your brother?"

The school of Malik and the people of Madina in this domain is closer to the *Sunna* and to justice than the school of those of the people of Kufa and others who oppose them. That is because their opponents consider that the sale is permitted when it

1. *Mulamasa* is a sale by touch without seeing the goods and *munabadha* a type of sale without inspection of the goods.
2. A sale which involves the sale of an unborn animal.

involves something which is present, whether its soundness has appeared or not appeared. They say that every contract entails the consequence of taking possession of the thing sold and they do not permit any delay in taking possession. They say that when someone buys the fruit, whether or not their soundness has appeared, that is allowed and the contract is immediately binding. There is no allowance for him to delay until the soundness of the fruits appears, and he is not permitted to stipulate that. They make taking possession something which transfers responsibility onto the buyer from the seller. They go further than that and say, "When someone sells goods on hire, it is not sound to delay surrender of the goods." They say, "When he makes an exception for the use of the thing sold, like using the back of a camel [to ride] and living in a house, that is not permitted." All of that is a branch based on that analogy.

The people of Madina and the people of hadith differ from them in respect of all that and they follow the sound texts and that is in harmony with the sound just analogy. The one who says: "The contract entails the consequence of taking possession of the thing sold," is told, "What the contract entails is either learned from the Lawgiver [the Prophet] or from the aim of the one who actually makes the contract. There is nothing in the words of the Lawgiver which entails that this demands that the obligation of the contract be absolute. As for the two who make the contract, they are subject to what they agree to and they make the contract on that basis. Sometimes they may make a contract which demands its immediate conclusion, and sometimes it is based on the taking possession being delayed, as in the case of fruits. The absolute contract entails immediate effect, but they can delay it if there is benefit in the delay. It is like that with goods. When the goods sold contain benefit for the seller or someone else, like a tree whose fruit has appeared, or like an article which exists or like something about which the seller stipulates a clause that he can use it for a time, this contract does not entail that the buyer take what is not yet his and what he does not own since if he was able to sell only part of the object, he would be able to sell it without the use of it."

Then it is similarly said that if the buyer takes the goods or does not take them immediately, that is not harmful. Taking possession in the sale is not part of the conclusion of the contract as is the case in respect of pledges. As a consequence ownership is acquired before the buyer takes possession, and any increase in the value of thing sold belongs to him without dispute, even if it is still in the possession of the seller. However, the effect of taking possession is either in the taking on of responsibility or in the permission to dispose of it. It is confirmed that Ibn 'Umar said: "The effective *Sunna* is that anything on which a handshake takes place while it is alive and whole becomes the responsibility of the buyer."

This is what the people of Madina and the people of hadith believe. That responsibility should be connected to the ability to take possession is better than its being connected to the actual taking possession. This is what the *Sunna* says. When fruits have been afflicted by disease, the buyer cannot harvest them, and is therefore absolved from the sale. If they are spoiled, it is the liability of the seller. This is also why, if the spoiling takes place during the time when the buyer delays taking possession, it becomes his liability. The slave and beast which can be taken are also his liability, based on the hadith reported by 'Ali and Ibn 'Umar.

If anyone makes disposal contingent on liability he has erred. There is agreement that if something for hire is destroyed before the hirer can have full use of it, it remains the liability of the lessor while the hirer has to pay a fee appropriate for the amount of his use of it. They disagree about a thing being hired out again for more than the original charge in case that becomes a profit gained from something in respect of which there is no liability. The correct position, however, is that it is permitted to do that because it becomes the liability of the original hirer. If it becomes unusable after he has been able to make full use of it, then it is his liability, but if it becomes unusable before he has been able to make full use of it, then it is not his liability.

This is the basis of the matter. It is established in the *Sahih* that Ibn 'Umar said, "We used to buy food without it being weighed or measured in the time of the Messenger of Allah, may Allah bless him and grant him peace, but he forbade us to re-sell it until we had transferred it to our animals." Ibn 'Umar is the one who said, "The effective *Sunna* is that anything on which a handshake takes place while it is alive and whole becomes the responsibility of the buyer," so it is clear that things like this food become the buyer's responsibility and he cannot sell it until he has moved it. He can dispose of the yield of the fruit tree and its produce. If it is destroyed before he is able to take possession of it, it is the liability of the lessor and seller, as the benefits can only be disposed of after he has them in full. Similarly fruits are not sold as if on the trees after having been cut which is not the case with food which is capable of being transferred.

The *Sunna* concerning this subject makes a distinction between the person who is able to take possession and the person who is not able to take possession in respect of liability and disposal. The people of Madina follow the *Sunna* more closely in all of this and their position is more equitable than the statement of those who oppose the *Sunna*.

There are many similar things, such as selling goods which are not actually present. Some of the *fuqaha'* absolutely permit their sale, even if they have not been described, and some forbid their sale even when they are described. Malik permits their sale when they are described but not when they are not, and this is more equitable.

In contracts, some people oblige precise articulation of them and the immediate succession of the offer and its acceptance and such things. The people of Madina make the starting point in contracts derive from the customs and habits of the people of the place where they take place. What the people consider to be a sale is a sale and what they consider to be hire is hire and what they consider to be a gift is a gift. This is closer to the Book and the *Sunna* and more just.

Some terms have a linguistic definition, like sun and moon, while others have a definition in the *Shari'a*, like prayer and hajj. Still others have no definition either linguistically or in the *Shari'a*, but rather refer to customs, like taking possession (*qabd*). It is known that the terms, "sale," "hire" and "gift" in this area were not defined by the Lawgiver nor do they have a linguistic definition. Rather their definition varies according to the customs and habits of the people concerned. So what they consider to be a sale is a sale and what they consider to be a gift is a gift and what they consider to be hire is hire.

On the same basis Malik permitted the sale of things which are still buried in the ground, such as carrots and turnips and the sale of cucumbers in general, and he and the group permitted the sale of beans and the like in their pods. There is no doubt that this was what the Muslims in the time of their Prophet, may Allah bless him and grant him peace, used to do and it has continued up until now. The best interests of people are not served except in this way. He does not consider this as a type of uncertainty. Therefore things such as this are permitted in other sales because it is both a question of ease and also something made necessary by need. Either ease or need on their own would make it allowed, so how much more so when they both exist!

It is the same when Malik makes the use of trees subordinate to the use of land, as in the case of renting land or a house where there is a tree or two. This is closer to the basic principles than the statement of those who forbid that. A group of the companions of Ahmad ibn Hanbal permitted it absolutely.

The Madinans allow a debt to be settled by a garden which contains land and trees, as 'Umar ibn al-Khattab did when he accepted a third of the garden from Usayd ibn al-Hudayr and he settled the debt that he had advanced him which he still owed him. I have discussed this question extensively elsewhere.

This subject will be made even clearer by mentioning usury. Its prohibition is stronger than the prohibition of gambling because it is an unquestionable injustice. When Allah – glory be to Him and may He be exalted – arranged His creation into two types – rich and poor – He made it obligatory for the rich to pay *zakat* as a duty to benefit the poor and He forbade the rich to practise usury which injures the poor. The Almighty says, *"Allah obliterates usury but makes* sadaqa *increase in value,"* (2:274) and He says, *"What you give with usurious intent, aiming to get back a greater amount from people's wealth does not become greater with Allah. But anything you give as* zakat, *seeking the Face of Allah – all who do that will get back twice as much."* (30:39) Those who are unjust refuse to pay *zakat* and then consume usury.

As for gambling, each of the gamblers wagers against the other, and the loser may be rich, or both gamblers may be equal in wealth or poverty. A gambler consumes money worthlessly and therefore Allah forbade it. Gambling does not, however, entail the same injustice and injury against the needy that usury entails. It is known that injustice towards the needy is more severe than injustice towards those who are not in need.

It is known that the people of Madina made usury unlawful and they forbade all devices (*hiyal*) used to make it lawful and they cut off the means which lead to it. Where is this in relation to the one who allows the devices used to take it? In fact that is directing people to do it. This will become evident by mentioning examples of straight usury [*riba al-fadl*] and usury arising out of delay of payment [*riba an-nasi'a*].

As for straight usury, it is established in sound *hadiths* and the Companions, Followers and four Imams agree that gold, silver, wheat, barley, dates and raisins cannot be sold in the same category except like for like. If there is any increase when like is exchanged for like, that is consuming property falsely, and it is injustice. When someone with a debt wants to sell a hundred broken dinars of one kind whose weight comes to 120 dinars of another kind, then the people who allow these enabling devices allow him to attribute that sale to a loaf of bread or handkerchief in which he puts the hundred dinars, and they allow other similar things which make it easy for every usurer to act. So the prohibition of usury is then valueless and pointless, for if a usurer wishes to sell any of these categories for a greater amount of the same category, he only has to add to it a little of something which is not reckoned in these matters.

It is the same when they are allowed delay so that a man sells someone else goods for which the buyer has no desire and then they are bought back from him for a higher price. The tricks they use allow anyone who desires to practise usury to do so.

It is known that if the Messenger made something unlawful, that thing contains corruption (*fasâd*) and that to permit it to be done by any means whatsoever has no benefit in it. So to do this is a fault and stupidity. The corruption is still there, but it has increased by their cheating. And if that involves inconvenience to themselves, they have put themselves out and gained no benefit at all. And what does such a person think of the Messenger, may Allah bless him and grant him peace? Indeed it is known that if a king was to forbid something which the Prophet forbade and then the person who was forbidden that thing then used a trick which was not forbidden in this sort of way, they would have considered him a cheater who was mocking their commands. Allah punished the people of the garden[1] who devised a stratagem to avoid paying *zakat*, and Allah punished the village which was near the sea[2] when they made the forbidden lawful by a trick and He transformed its inhabitants into apes and pigs. It has come that the Prophet, may Allah bless him and grant him peace, said, "Do not do what the Jews did. They made lawful what Allah made unlawful by the worst kind of trickery."

---

1. Qur'an (68:17-33).
2. Qur'an (7: 163-167).

We have discussed that extensively in *The Principle of the Invalidity of Devices and on the Stopping of Means*, in a single large volume. In it we confirmed the school of the people of Madina on the basis of the Book and the *Sunna* and the consensus of the first generation of the Muhajirun and the Ansar.

It is the same in the case of usury involving delay. Among the people of the tribe of Thaqif, and it was about them that the Qur'an was sent down, a man used to go to his debtor when repayment of the debt was due and say, "Will you pay it off or pay an increase?" If he did not pay him, the creditor got more money and the debtor a longer term, and so the money became doubled over the period because of the delay. This is usury about which there is no doubt by the agreement of all the *Salaf* of the community. The Qur'anic *ayats* were revealed about it and the injustice and injury inherent in it are clear.

Allah – glory be to Him and may He be exalted – made selling lawful and trade lawful and He made usury unlawful. The buyer buys things for his own use such as food, clothes, dwellings, mounts, etc., and the merchant buys things he wants to sell in order to make a profit from them. As for practising usury, its aim is to lend dirhams for dirhams over a set term, and the usurer then demands more than the amount lent without having conferred any benefit and without any selling or trading. The usurer consumes money wrongly with injustice and the people do not benefit from him by trade or anything else. Rather he lends his dirhams to obtain an increase which is without any benefit either for him or other people.

When this is their intention, then by whatever means it is attained, the result is corruption and injustice, as for instance when a man is granted a delay so that he can buy something and then sell it, which amounts to two sales in one sale. In the *Sunan* the Prophet, may Allah bless him and grant him peace, said, "Whoever makes two sales in one sale, should take the lesser of the two or it is usury." It is as if an imaginary middle-man, to make the transaction permissible, is interposed between the two

49

sales. Then the usurer buys something he has no desire for so that he can sell it again to the one who is paying the usury, who then returns it to the imaginary middle-man for a lesser price.

It is established from the Prophet, may Allah bless him and grant him peace, that he cursed the one who consumed usury and the one who paid it and its witness and its scribe. He cursed the one who makes something [unlawful] permissible and the thing he makes permissible for instance someone who combines a loan with usury when it is established that the Prophet said, "It is not lawful to have a sale with delayed payment for more than the cash price, nor two preconditions in one sale, nor profit on something not yet in your possession [i.e. nebulous and indefinite], nor selling what you do not have."

Then the Prophet, may Allah bless him and grant him peace, forbade the *muzâbana* and the *muhâqala* sales which involve the buying of dates and grain by guessing their amount, and he also forbade selling an unmeasured heap of food for a measured amount of food because there is ignorance of the equivalence in a situation where equality is a precondition, so knowledge of the difference is essential. Guessing is no gauge of the amount of the measure since it is only surmise and conjecture. This is agreed upon by all the Imams.

Then it is confirmed from the Prophet that he allowed the people with *'ariyyas* [when someone has the use of date-palms but not their ownership] to sell by estimating the amount of their dates and so he permitted such a sale here by guesswork, and thus guesswork can take the place of measuring if there is a real need. This is part of the perfection of the splendour of the *Shari'a*, as is also the case in the science of *zakat* and its division where guesswork can take the place of measuring. The Prophet used to estimate the fruits when *zakat* was collected. 'Abdullah ibn Rawaha divided up for the people of Khaybar by estimate at the command of the Prophet. It is known that when it is possible to determine by measuring, that is what is done. When it is not possible, then estimating takes its place through need, as is the case with all other customary substitutes. For instance analogy takes the place of the text when there is none, and evaluation takes the place of the equivalent when none is available and the price of the original article is not known.

✳✳✳✳✳

Connected with this is the science of physiognomy, which is deducing lineage by likeness when deduction by circumstances is impossible, since the child roughly resembles his father. Physiognomy and evaluation are substitutes in knowledge just as analogy is a substitute for the text. That is how it is with justice in action. The *Shari'a* is based on doing justice, as the Almighty says, *"We sent Our Messengers with the Clear Signs and sent down the Book and the Balance with them so that mankind might establish justice,"* (57:25) and *"Allah does not impose on any self any more than it can stand."* (2:283)

Allah has prescribed retaliation with respect to lives, property and honour according to what is possible in the circumstances. The Almighty says, *"Retaliation has been prescribed for you in the case of people killed..."* (2:177) and the Almighty says, *"We prescribed for them in it a life for a life ..."* (5:47) The Almighty says, *"The repayment of a bad action is one equivalent to it..."* (42:40) The Almighty says, *"So if anyone oversteps the limits against you, overstep against him the same as he did to you."* (2:193) The Almighty says *"If you want to retaliate, retaliate to the same degree as the injury done to you..."* (16:126)

So when a man kills someone who is his peer deliberately out of aggression towards him, retaliation is taken against him. It is permitted for the same as he did to be done to him, and this is the position of the people of Madina and those who agree with them, like ash-Shafi'i and Ibn Hanbal, in one of two transmissions, according to what is possible in the circumstances and when it is not forbidden by the right of Allah. An example of this is the crushing of the culprit's head as the Prophet, may Allah

51

bless him and grant him peace, did when he ordered the crushing of the head of the Jew who had crushed the head of a girl. That is more complete in respect of justice than killing him by cutting off his head with the sword. When retaliation is impossible, then one turns to blood-money, and blood-money is a replacement when doing the same thing is impossible.

If someone destroys another person's property, for instance when the *'ariyya* in his possession is destroyed, then he owes something equivalent to it if he has such a thing. If he doesn't have it, then he owes the price of it in dirhams and dinars, and this acts as a substitute when the equivalent is not available. This is why someone who insists on the equivalent of things, according to what is possible in the circumstances, while at the same time taking the price into consideration as well, is closer to justice than the one who insists on the price without taking the equivalent of a thing into consideration at all. This is dealt with by the [Qur'anic] story of Da'ud and Sulayman, which we discussed earlier.[1] Our aim here is simply to call attention to it.

Then the permission for the *'ariyya* to be sold by estimation is only granted in cases of actual need when it is impossible to sell them by the measure demanded by the principles of the *Shari'a* and it also has the affirmation of the sound *Sunna*. It is the school of the people of Madina and the people of hadith. Malik permitted estimation in such cases when there is actual need. This is the essence of sound *fiqh*.

The school of the people of Madina and those who agree with them, like ash-Shafi'i and Ahmad ibn Hanbal, is that the penalty for game [i.e. game killed while in *ihram*] is that the person is liable for its equivalent in size, as exemplified by the *Sunna* and the judgements of the Companions. The Prophet, may Allah bless him and grant him peace, decided on a ram for a hyena and the Companions decided on a camel for an ostrich, and a sheep for a gazelle, and so on.

---

1. p. 12.

Those who opposed them among the people of Kufa insisted on a monetary equivalent as the penalty for game and that the person involved has to buy any kind of livestock with it even though the price varies at different times.

Section: Unlawful business behaviour

Just as there are two types of unlawful things: one being the thing in itself and the other being unlawful by acquisition, so there are two categories of acquisition, which lies in the behaviour of people: viz. exchange and partnership. Buying and selling and hiring and such things constitute exchange. As for partnership, it consists of things like the *'inan* (limited[1]) and other kinds of partnership.

Malik's school concerning partnerships is the soundest and most just of them. He permits the *'inan* [limited] partnership and the *abdân* partnership [in work] and other forms of partnership. He permits *mudâraba* [*qirad* or *commenda*], *muzâra'a* [sharecropping with labour in exchange for produce] and *musâqa* [sharecropping on its own (as distinct from *muzâra'a*)].

Ash-Shafi'i only permits those partnerships which are in accordance with the partnerships of Malik. Partnership consists of two types: partnership in respect of property and partnership in respect of contracts. Partnership in respect of property is like that of heirs who share in an inheritance and has no need of any contract. But when two people share in a contract, the school of ash-Shafi'i is that the partnership is only formed by the existence of an actual contract and division can only be made according to that contract.

Ibn Hanbal also considers that a partnership is formed by a contract and that the division takes place according to the contract and he permits *'inan* partnership when there are two different properties as long as they are not mixed together. When the two partners settle the account, he thinks that it can be without partition in kind. So even if property decreases after that, it does not bring about a reduction in the profit.

Ash-Shafi'i does not permit the *abdân* partnership or the *wujûh* or a partnership without the mixing together of two prop-

---

1. Partnership in one particular item.

erties nor does he stipulate a precondition of profit for one of them above the share of the other from his property since he considers that it has no effect on the contract. He permits *mudâraba* and some *musâqa* and *muzâra'a* in case of need, but not by analogy.

Abu Hanifa himself does not permit *musaqa* or *muzara'a* because he deems that to be a branch of hiring and hiring must involve a specified wage.

Malik takes a broader view than both of them regarding this since he allows *musâqa* on all fruits and also allows various other types of partnerships, i.e. the *'inan* partnership and *abdân*. But he does not allow the *muzâra'a* sharecropping agreement in the case of barren land which is in agreement with the Kufans.

As for the early people of Madina and others among the Companions and Followers, they used to permit all these things. That is the position of al-Layth, Ibn Abi Layla, Abu Yusuf and Muhammad ash-Shaybani and the *fuqaha'* of hadith like Ahmad ibn Hanbal and others.

The doubt which prevents people agreeing to these transactions is that they think that they amount to hire and hire inevitably involves a specified wage. They make an exception in the case of *mudâraba* because of need since dirhams cannot be hired.

The correct position is that all these transactions are partnerships and do not amount to exchanges. Anyone who hires intends full use of work as is the case with tailors, bakers, cooks and the like. In these other transactions, work is not the intention. Rather one person gives the use of his body and the other the use of his property so that they share in whatever profit Allah gives them. Either they both gain or they both lose. This is the basis on which the Prophet, may Allah bless him and grant him peace, employed the people of Khaybar on the basis that they were to cultivate the land at their own expense for half of the fruit and produce it yielded.

The thing which the Prophet, may Allah bless him and grant him peace, forbade in the *muzâra'a* type of renting agricultural land in the hadith of Rafi' ibn Khadij and others is agreed upon, as al-Layth and others mentioned. He forbade the renting of land in return for the produce growing along irrigation canals and brooks in it plus a certain amount of figs. Perhaps these plants would yield and those plants not yield. So he forbade the owner to stipulate the produce of a certain area as he forbade in *mudâraba* that the agent stipulate a certain fixed sum from the profit or the profit from certain specific garments because that would nullify the equity of the partnership.

The premise of the people of Madina regarding this matter is sounder than that of others who say that a wage is necessary. The first is the correct position. The contract is not based on work. This is why knowledge of the work done is not specified. It is possible that the wage might exceed both the capital and its profit and he would also be due from an unsound transaction the same as he would be due from a sound one. If a price is obligatory for a valid sale and a wage for valid employment and a share of revenue in an unsound transaction is a prerequisite then a share in the revenue of something unsound becomes a prerequisite [which is clearly absurd]. That would be the case in the *musâqa* and *muzâra'a* and other similar transactions.

If there is some weakness in respect of this matter in the position of the later people of Madina, then the position of Kufans regarding it is weaker still. It seems that all of this arose from new opinions which were known by those of the *Salaf* who censured it. What has come down in the *Sunna* and *'amal* is true justice.

If anyone considers the basic premises, it will be clear to him that the *musâqa*, *muzâra'a* and *mudâraba* are closer to justice than hiring. Hiring is risky and the hirer can benefit or not benefit as opposed to the *musâqa* and *muzâra'a* in which the partners share in profit and loss. So there is no risk in it from either side as there is in the case of hire.

Section: there is no *deen* except what Allah pre-scribed and nothing unlawful except what Allah made unlawful.

As for acts of worship, the basic premise of the *deen* is that there is nothing unlawful except what Allah has made unlawful and there is no *deen* except what Allah has prescribed. In *Surat al-An'am* and *Surat al-A'raf,* Allah – glory be to Him – censured the idolaters because they made unlawful what Allah had not made unlawful and they prescribed in the *deen* things for which Allah had not given leave. It is as Ibn 'Abbas said, "If you want to recognise the ignorance of the Arabs, then read from His words, *'They assign to Allah a share of the crops and livestock...'"* (6:136) That is when Allah censured the idolaters for what they had innovated by making crops and animals unlawful and for what they had innovated of *shirk.* He censured them for arguing on behalf of their innovations using the Decree in defence of their arguments. The Almighty says, *"Those who associate others with Allah will say, 'If Allah had willed we would not have associated anything with Him...'"* (6:149)

In the *Sahih* Collection 'Iyad ibn Himar reported that the Prophet, may Allah bless him and grant him peace, said, "Allah Almighty says, 'I created My slaves with a natural inclination to belief and then the shaytans diverted them and made unlawful for them what I had made lawful and commanded them to associate with Me things for which I had not sent down authority.'"

The things they made unlawful and the things they prescribed are mentioned in *Surat al-A'raf.* Allah Almighty says, *"My Lord has forbidden indecency, both open and hidden ..."* (7:31)[1] and He says, *"Say: 'My Lord has commanded justice...'"* (7:28)[2] So it was clear to

1. *"Say: 'My Lord has forbidden indecency, both open and hidden, and wrong action, and unrightful tyranny, and associating anything with Allah for which He has sent down no authority, and saying things about Allah you do not know.'"*

2. *"Say: 'My Lord has commanded justice. Stand and face Him in mosques and call on Him, making your deen sincerely His. As He originated you, so you will return.' One group He guided; but another group get the misguidance they deserve.*

57

them that He did not command them to do those things nor did He make the other things unlawful. He said to censure them, *"Or do they have partners who have laid down a* deen *for them ...:"* (42:21) This has been fully dealt with elsewhere.

The point is that it is not for anyone to make unlawful anything except what the *Shari'a* says is unlawful. Otherwise the basic rule is that a thing is not unlawful, whether that be an item or an action. It is not for anyone to prescribe something as obligatory or recommended when there is no proof in the *Shari'a* of it being obligatory or recommended.

✷✷✷✷✷

Given this, then the people of Madina are the strongest of people in clinging to that basic premise. They are the strongest of the people of any of the Muslim cities in disliking innovations. We noted that other people made things and transactions unlawful which they did not. As for the *deen,* they are the strongest of the people of the cities in following the prescribed acts of worship and the furthest of them from any innovated acts of worship.

Examples of this are numerous. One is that a group of the Kufans and others recommended that a person doing *wudu'*, *ghusl,* praying, etc. should articulate the intention in these acts of worship and they state that articulating the intention is stronger than simply making the intention inwardly, even though none of the Imams made such an articulation obligatory. The people of Madina do not recommend that, and this is the correct course. The people of Ibn Hanbal have two views on it.

That is because this is an innovation which the Messenger of Allah, may Allah bless him and grant him peace, did not do and nor did his Companions. Rather he began the prayer with the *takbir* and did not utter any of these expressions before the *takbir*.

They took the shaytans as friends instead of Allah and thought that they were guided."

It is the same with his instruction of the Companions. He taught them to begin with the *takbir*. This articulation is an innovation in the *Shari'a* and it is also an error in the intention. The intention for an action is a necessary matter in the heart and the articulation of it has no value, like the one eating articulating the intention to eat and the one drinking, the intention to drink and the one having intercourse, the intention to have intercourse and the traveller the intention to travel and things like that.

Another example is found in the constituents of the acts of worship. Malik and the people of Madina do not permit altering any constituent of the prescribed acts of worship. So the prayer is not begun without the prescribed *takbir*, which is saying, *"Allahu akbar,"* and this *takbir* is what is prescribed in the *adhan* and the *'ids*. They do not permit the Qur'an being recited [in the prayer] in other than Arabic. They do not permit any deviation from what is stipulated as being intended by *zakat* in favour of something the owner might prefer to have taken of his property when it is in accord with the required value.

With regard to the times of the prayer they follow the *Sunna* more closely than the people of Kufa since they recommend praying *Fajr* and *'Asr* at the beginning of their time and say that the time of *'Asr* is when the shadow of a thing is equal to it which marks the end of the time of *Dhuhr*. They make the time of the *'Isha'* and *Maghrib* prayers shared for someone who has an excuse, such as a menstruating woman when she becomes pure of menstruation and a mad person when he recovers his senses. They also permit a traveller hastening in his journey to join the prayers together, and also allow this for a sick person and in case of heavy rain.

They are balanced about the travelling prayer. There are some *fuqaha'* who consider the full prayer better than shortening it, or consider shortening it better though without disliking the full prayer and saying you should not shorten unless you have made an intention to do so. Some of them, on the other hand, consider that it is not permitted to make the full prayer. They [the people of Madina] think that the *Sunna* is shortening and it is disliked to do four *rak'ats*. They make shortening a firm *sunna* (*sunna ratiba*), and joining the prayers a non-essential allowance. There is no doubt that this position is the closest position to the *Sunna*.

Similarly, they consider the *witr* with a single *rak'at* one of the firm *sunnas*, and pray the *shaf'* before it. This is sounder than the position of the Kufans who say that there is no *witr* except in the form of *Maghrib*. It is sound to allow both of them, but making a division between the *shaf'* and *witr* is better than combining them. So the position of the Madinans is preferred absolutely to the position of the Kufans. The Madinans also do not think that there is a firm *sunna* prayer before *Jumu'a* differing by this from those of the Kufans who oppose them.

Malik did not fix the time for any other than the obligatory prayers, whereas some of the Iraqis fixed the times for them using weak hadiths. So the position of Malik is closer to the *Sunna* in this as well.

✳✳✳✳✳

The people of Madina think that someone performing hajj should combine the prayers at 'Arafa, and Muzdalifa, and shorten them at Mina, no matter whether he is one of the people of Makka or not. There is no doubt that this was the *Sunna* of the Messenger of Allah, may Allah bless him and grant him peace. This is one of the positions in the schools of ash-Shafi'i and Ahmad ibn Hanbal. The position of those who say that it is only permitted to shorten for the person among them who has travelled the distance normally required for shortening is contrary to the *Sunna*.

Those of the people of Iraq and others who make these statements think that the Prophet, may Allah bless him and grant him peace, prayed at Mina and then said, "O people of Makka, complete your prayer. We are a people who are travelling." This is falsely attributed to the Prophet, may Allah bless him and grant him peace, by the agreement of the people of hadith. It is recorded in the *Sunan* that he made this statement when he prayed in Makka during the Conquest. They similarly transmitted this from 'Umar.

It is related that when Harun ar-Rashid performed the *hajj*, he ordered Abu Yusuf to lead the people in prayer. When he said the *salam*, he said, "O people of Makka, complete your prayer. We are a people who are travelling." One of the Makkans said to him, "Do you tell us this when the *Sunna* emerged from among us?" He retorted, "Is this part of your *fiqh* – that you speak while you are in the prayer?"

Speaking out of forgetfulness or out of ignorance that speech is forbidden does not invalidate the prayer according Malik, ash-Shafi'i and Ibn Hanbal. But it does invalidate it according to Abu Hanifa. If the Makkan had known the *Sunna*, he would have said, "This is not the *Sunna*. The Prophet, may Allah bless him and grant him peace, prayed two *rak'ats* at Mina as did Abu Bakr and 'Umar, as they prayed two *rak'ats* at 'Arafa and Muzdalifa, and they did not command the Makkans behind them to do the full prayer in it." Such is the school of the people of Madina.

Another point of dispute is found in the eclipse prayer. The *Sunan* collections have transmitted by multiple transmissions that the Prophet, may Allah bless him and grant him peace, prayed it with two bowings in each *rak'at*, and the people of Madina follow this *sunna* more closely. It was unknown to the people of Kufa and so they denied it.

It is the same with the rain prayer. It is established in sound hadiths that the Prophet, may Allah bless him and grant him peace, prayed the rain prayer and the people of Madina saw him perform it to ask for rain. This *sunna* is unknown to those among the people of Iraq who object to the rain prayer.

Another matter are the extra *takbirs* of the *'id*. The bulk of the *Sunan* collections and traditions agree with the school of the people of Madina that there are seven *takbirs* of opening, including the *takbir al-ihram*, in the first and five in the second.

✳✳✳✳✳

Another thing is regarding whether you can catch the prayer by a *rak'at* or less than a *rak'at*. The school of Malik is that you catch it with a *rak'at*. This is what is sound in its transmission from the Prophet, may Allah bless him and grant him peace, since he said, "Whoever catches a *rak'at* of the prayer has caught the prayer." He said, "Whoever catches a *rak'at* of *Fajr* before the sun rises has caught it. Whoever catches a *rak'at* of *'Asr* before the sun sets has caught *'Asr*." Malik says that the *Jumu'a* and any group prayer is caught by doing one *rak'at*. Similarly the prayer can be caught at the end of its time. It is like that with catching the time as in the case of a menstruating woman when she becomes pure and a mad person when he recovers his sanity before the time has gone.

Abu Hanifa makes catching the prayer in all the prayers dependent on catching just a single *takbir*, and he even says about the *Jumu'a*, "If someone catches even a single *takbir* of it, he has caught it." Ash-Shafi'i and Ahmad ibn Hanbal agree with Malik about *Jumu'a* but differ about other prayers. Most of their people agree with Abu Hanifa about the rest. It is known that the position of the one who agrees with Malik in all of them is sounder both in respect of text and analogy.

Some of them use as an argument against Malik the words of the Prophet in the sound *hadith*, "Whoever catches a prostration of the prayer," but this is not a valid argument because what is meant by "prostration" in this instance is the *rak'at* as Ibn 'Umar says, "I memorised from the Messenger of Allah, may Allah bless him and grant him peace, 'Two *rak'ats* before *Dhuhr* and two prostrations after it.'" Such examples are numerous.

Another thing is that in the school of the people of Madina, when the Imam prays forgetting that he is in *janaba* or *hadath* [i.e. needs to do a *ghusl* or *wudu*] and then remembers, he repeats the prayer but those who followed him do not have to repeat it. This is transmitted from the Rightly-guided Khalifs like 'Umar and 'Uthman. Abu Hanifa thinks that everyone should repeat the prayer. That is mentioned by one transmission from Ibn Hanbal, but the well-known position from him is the same as the position of Malik. And that is also the school of ash-Shafi'i and others.

Another thing supporting this position is an incident that took place with Abu Yusuf. The khalif had delegated him to perform the *Jumu'a* prayer and he led the people in the prayer and then he remembered that he had broken his *wudu*'. So he repeated the prayer but did not command the people to repeat it. He was asked about that and he said, "Perhaps that would constrict them, and so we took the position of our Madinan brothers." There is much disagreement about the *Jumu'a* prayer since having an Imam is a precondition for it.

On the same basis, Malik also disregards all the errors of the Imam. When the Imam prays according to his *ijtihad* and omits something that the person praying behind him considers to be obligatory, such as not thinking that it is obligatory to recite the *basmala*, or that *wudu*' is not necessary on account of blood or loud laughter or after touching women, when the person praying behind him thinks that those things are obligatory, the school of Malik says that the prayer of the person following is sound. This is one of the two positions taken by Ibn Hanbal and ash-Shafi'i, and the other position, which is that of Abu Hanifa, is not sound.

The school of the people of Madina with regard to this matter is the one whose soundness is undoubted. It is established in the *Sahih* Collection of al-Bukhari that the Prophet, may Allah bless him and grant him peace, said, "They lead you in the prayer. If they are correct, it is for you and for them. It they err, it is for you but against them." This is explicit in respect of the question concerned. Since the Imam prays by his *ijtihad*, his prayer is not judged to be invalid. Do you not think that his judgement would be enforced when he judged according to his *ijtihad*? So being led by him as an Imam is more proper.

Anyone who disputes this bases his disagreement on the fact that the person following the Imam believes the prayer of the Imam to be invalid. This is an error. The Imam prayed by his *ijtihad* or by his imitation (*taqlid*). If he is correct, he has two rewards. If he erred, he has one reward and his error is forgiven, so how can it be said that his prayer is invalid?

Then it is known by multiple transmission from the *Salaf* of the community that they continued to pray behind one another even though differences of that sort existed. Thus ash-Shafi'i and those like him continued to pray behind the people of Madina even though the Madinans did not recite the *basmala* either silently or aloud.

It is transmitted that Harun ar-Rashid was cupped and he asked Malik for a *fatwa* and he gave him a *fatwa* that he did not have to do *wudu'* and Abu Yusuf prayed behind him. The school of Abu Hanifa and Ibn Hanbal is that the emergence of impurity by other than the two normal means invalidates *wudu'* and the position of Malik and ash-Shafi'i is that it does not invalidate *wudu'*. Abu Yusuf was asked, "Why do you then pray behind him?" He said, "Glory be to Allah! The Amir al-Mu'minin!"

Not praying behind the Imams for something like this is one of the signs of the people of innovations like the Rafidites and the Mu'tazilites. This is why when Imam Ahmad ibn Hanbal was asked about this, he gave a *fatwa* that *wudu'* was obligatory for bleeding. The asker said to him, "If the Imam does not do *wudu'*, can I still pray behind him?" He said, "Glory be to Allah! Would you not pray behind Sa'id ibn al-Musayyab and Malik ibn Anas?"

Malik thought that the speech of the one who forgets or is ignorant in the prayer does not invalidate it, based on the hadith of Dhu'l-Yadayn, the hadith of Mu'awiya ibn al-Hakam when he blessed the one who sneezed, and the hadith of the bedouin who said in the prayer, "O Allah, show mercy on me and Muhammad and do not show mercy on anyone else besides us two!"

This is the position of ash-Shafi'i and Ibn Hanbal in one of two transmissions and the other transmission is the same as the position of Abu Hanifa. They say that the hadith of Dhu'l-Yadayn occurred before speech was forbidden, but that is not the case. The hadith of Dhu'l-Yadyan was reported after Khaybar since Abu Hurayra witnessed it and Abu Hurayra only became Muslim in the year of Khaybar. The prohibition of speech took place before Ibn Mas'ud returned from Abyssinia and Ibn Mas'ud was present at Badr!

The school of the people of Madina regarding supplication in the prayer, cautioning by the Qur'an, and saying "Glory be to Allah," and that sort of thing is part of the amplitude allowed in respect of things about which the *Sunna* is in agreement which is contrary to the position of the Kufans who are very constricted indeed regarding this matter and make all those things speech which is forbidden in the prayer.

Another thing with regard to purification is that Malik thought that *wudu'* is necessary on account of touching the penis and on account of touching women with desire, but not for laughing in the prayer and touching women without desire. There is also *wudu'* for something unusual which emerges from the two normal places and the emergence of impurity from other than them. Abu Hanifa thought that *wudu'* is necessary for laughing out loud and for the emergence of any impurity at all from either place, but he did not think it need be done for touching the penis.

It is known that the hadiths about touching the penis invalidating *wudu'* are firmer and better known than the hadiths about loud laughter, which no one related in the *Sunan* collections at all. They are considered by the people of hadith to be weak *mursal* hadiths, and this is why none of the people of hadith make *wudu'* obligatory on account of loud laughter since they know that nothing about it is established with them.

There are three well-known positions about touching women. The position of Abu Hanifa is that there is no need for *wudu'* for that in any instance. The position of Malik and the people of Madina, which is also the best known one from Ibn Hanbal, is that if it is done with desire, then *wudu'* is broken. Otherwise it is not broken. The position of ash-Shafi'i is that *wudu'* must be done for it in any case.

There is no doubt that the position of Abu Hanifa and the position of Malik are the two well-known positions among the *Salaf*. As for making it obligatory for someone who touches women without desire to do *wudu'*, it is an odd position with no basis in either the Book or in the *Sunna* or in a tradition from any of the *Salaf* of the community, and it does not accord with the fundamental principles of the *Shari'a*. A touch which is free of desire does not have any effect on either *ihram* nor *i'tikaf*, in the way that touching with desire does have an effect on them. It is not something which it is disliked for someone fasting to do nor does it entail marital relations nor effect any of the actions of worship or any other legal judgement.

Anyone who makes it break purity opposes fundamental principles. When Allah says, *"If you have touched women"* (4:43; 5:6), He only means intercourse by that as 'Umar and others have said. It is known that His words, *"or you have touched"* refers to *wudu'*. It is the same with His words about *i'tikaf*, *"But do not have sexual intercourse* [lit. *bâshara*, to touch] *with them while you are in retreat in the mosques."* (2:186) Touching without desire has no effect there, and so it is also the case here. It is like His words, *"If you divorce them before you have touched them."* (2:235)

Moreover we know that men continue to touch women without desire. If that had made *wudu'*, necessary the Messenger of Allah, may Allah bless him and grant him peace, would have commanded the Muslims to do it, and it would have been part of what was transmitted and reported.

This is similar to the argument that some people use against Malik regarding the question of sperm, namely that people also continue to have wet dreams and thus their bodies and clothes become *junub*. If *ghusl* had been obligatory, then the Prophet, may Allah bless him and grant him peace, would have command-ed it. However, he did not command any of the Muslims to wash off whatever sperm got onto his clothes or his body although he did command menstruating women to wash the menstrual blood from their clothes. It is well-known that the impurity of *janaba* affects the people's clothes more than menstrual blood does those of women, so why did he make washing clear in the case menstruating women and not in the other case in order to give clarification of that general principle?

It is not permitted to explain this away by saying that the time of need for it did not arise and what is established in the *Sahih* Collection about 'A'isha washing the sperm from the Prophet's garment does not indicate any obligation. It is also confirmed in the *Sahih* that she used to rub over it with water. Sa'd ibn Abi Waqqas and Ibn 'Abbas said, "Remove it from you, even by fumi-gation." Sperm has the same status as mucus and saliva.

The same applies to performing *ghusl* for *janaba*. The school of Malik and one of the positions of the school of Ibn Hanbal, the one, in fact, which is transmitted from him and by which the *Sunna* is followed, follows the transmission regarding the *ghusl* of the Messenger of Allah, may Allah bless him and grant him peace, taken from such sources as 'A'isha and Maymuna. It is not transmitted that he washed his entire body three times. It is men-tioned that after doing *wudu'* and letting the water penetrate to the roots of the hair, he poured it over his head and then let the water flow over on the rest of his body after that.

Those who recommend doing it three times only do so by analogy based on the performance of *wudu'*. The *Sunna* makes a clear distinction between them. It is affirmed that the Prophet, may Allah bless him and grant him peace, used to do *wudu'* with a *mudd* of water and *ghusl* with a *sa'* of water, which is four *mudds*. It is known that if the *Sunna* for the *ghusl* had been to wash three times, that would not have been enough.

Another thing is *tayammum*. Some people say, like Abu Hanifa, that it is not obligatory to do *tayammum* for every prayer.

Some of them say that you must do *tayammum* for every prayer and this is the position of ash-Shafi'i. The school of Malik is that you have to do *tayammum* for every obligatory prayer. This is the justest of the positions, and it is closer to the traditions related from the Companions and is also what is related about women with bleeding outside normal menstruation.

※※※※※

Another thing is that the people of Madina make *zakat* obligatory on the property of co-owners, in the same way as they do on the property of sole owners. In respect of camels, when there are more than 120 of them, they make it a two year old for every forty, and a three year old for every fifty. This is in accordance with the letter of the Prophet, may Allah bless him and grant him peace, concerning *zakat,* which al-Bukhari transmitted from the hadith of Abu Bakr as-Siddiq, and the bulk of the letters of the Prophet on the same subject which were in the possession of the family of 'Umar ibn al-Khattab and the family of 'Ali ibn Abi Talib and others which are in agreement with this position.

Those of the Kufans who oppose them re-start the calculation for *zakat* in respect of each individual owner and co-ownership is not taken into account. They possess traditions on the subject of re-starting, but they do not have equal status to those of the Madinans. Even if there is confirmation of their position, it has been abrogated in the same way that the *zakat* of cattle being paid in sheep was abrogated.

The school of the people of Madina does not take *waqs* [amount over the minimum] into consideration except in respect of herd animals and gold and silver which exceed the minimum amount on which *zakat* must be paid, and that accords with what is related on that subject in tradition. Abu Hanifa makes the *waqs* follow in its particular category. So he thinks that there is no *zakat* on the *waqs* in respect of the two metals, gold and silver, just as there is none in respect of animals. As for the agricultural tenths, he believes that there is no *waqs* and no minimum (*nisab*), but says it is obligatory to pay a tenth (*'ushr*) in respect of all vegetables, whether a little or a lot.

His two companions, however, agree with the people of Madina, it being established that the Prophet, may Allah bless him and grant him peace, said "There is no *zakat* on anything less than five *wasqs*, and there is no *zakat* on what is less than five camels," and in what is established from him about not taking *zakat* from vegetables according to the words related from him, "There is no *zakat* on vegetables."

The position of the people of Madina about buried treasure about which the Prophet said, "There is a fifth on buried treasure," does not include mines. *Zakat* is obligatory on mines since it was taken from the mines of Bilal ibn al-Harith as Malik mentioned in his *Muwatta'*. [17:3] Anyone who ponders the *Muwatta'* and reflects on its interpretations and the traditions it contains and the way it is set out knows what is said by those of the people of Iraq who oppose it. The aim of that arrangement and the traditions included was to clarify the *Sunna* and to refute those who opposed it.

Any who have full knowledge of the respective positions of the people of Madina and Iraq also have full knowledge of the worth of the *Muwatta'*. This is why Malik remarked, "You learn a book which I compiled over the course of so many years in so many days. So how could you possibly understand what it contains?" The people of Iraq who differ from this consider that buried treasure is a category which includes both obtaining minerals by mining and what was buried in the *Jahiliyya*.

The same applies to the *hajj* practices. The people of Madina do not think that a person doing *qiran*[1] should do more than one *tawaf* and one *sa'y*. It is known that the sound hadiths from the Prophet, may Allah bless him and grant him peace, all agree with this position. The Kufans, however, believe that he should first do *tawaf* and *sa'y* for *'umra*, and then do *tawaf* and *sa'y* a second

---

1. Combining *hajj* and *'umra*.

time for the *hajj*. In saying this they adhere to the traditions transmitted from 'Ali and Ibn Mas'ud. Doing this is only correct if they are sound and do not contradict the sound *Sunna*.

The position of the people of Madina is that it is not recommended, and indeed is disliked, for someone to assume *ihram* before reaching the place of the *miqat*, whereas the Kufans recommend assuming *ihram* before it. However the position of the people of Madina agrees with the *Sunna* of the Messenger of Allah, may Allah bless him and grant him peace, and the *Sunna* of his Rightly-guided Khalifs.

Before the Farewell *Hajj*, the Prophet went on the '*Umra* of al-Hudaybiyya and the '*umra* of making up, and in both of them he assumed *ihram* at Dhu'l-Hulayfa. In the year of Hunayn he performed '*umra* from al-Ji'irrana, and then in the Farewell *Hajj* he went into *ihram* from Dhu'l-Hulayfa. He never assumed *ihram* from Madina in any of these instances. The Messenger of Allah, may Allah bless him and grant him peace, would not make a habit of abandoning the best practice. The khalifs after him, like 'Umar and 'Uthman, forbade people to assume *ihram* before the *miqat*.

Malik was asked about a man who assumed *ihram* before the *miqat* and he said, "I fear trouble for him." He said, "Allah Almighty says, *'Those who oppose His command should beware of a testing trial coming to them.'* (24:63)" The asker said, "What trouble could that be? It is just increase in obedience of Allah Almighty." He said, "And what trouble could be greater than supposing than you are singled out for an action which the Messenger of Allah, may Allah bless him and grant him peace, did not do?"

He used to say, "The last of this Community will not be put right except by what the first of it was put right with. Or are you saying that whenever a man comes to us with a stronger argument than another man, we should abandon what Jibril brought to Muhammad for the argument of this one?"

The position of the people of Madina is that if someone has sexual intercourse after 'Arafa before coming out of *ihram*, his hajj is invalidated; and if someone has sexual intercourse after coming out of *ihram* (before the *tawaf al-Ifada*) he owes an *'umra*. This is what was transmitted from the Companions as opposed to the position of those who say that sexual intercourse after 'Arafa does not invalidate the *hajj* and those who say that sexual intercourse after coming out of *ihram* does not oblige a second *'umra*. In saying that Malik followed the statement of Ibn 'Abbas. He mentioned it in his *Muwatta'* (20:50), but he did not name the person who transmitted it to him from Ibn 'Abbas since the transmitter of it was 'Ikrima. This was because it had also reached him from Ibn 'Umar and Sa'd.

If it is said that this position differs with the hadith of Duba'a bint az-Zubayr about coming out of *ihram* when she was prevented from completing the hajj, the hadith of 'A'isha about the Messenger of Allah putting on perfume before his *ihram* and before his *tawaf* of the House, and the hadith of Ibn 'Abbas about continuing the *talbiya* until stoning the *Jamra* of 'Aqaba and other things, it must be replied that when this is compared with what others among the Kufans and others disagree with, their disagreements are found to be much greater.

Moreover, regarding questions like these the Madinans tend to follow traditions from 'Umar ibn al-Khattab, Ibn 'Umar and others. When there is a dispute between the Companions, the correct course is to refer it to the *Sunna* of the Messenger of Allah, may Allah bless him and grant him peace. However, there are some who were missing some aspects of the *Sunna*, so it is preferable to follow 'Umar, Ibn 'Umar and those like them. The amount the Kufans do not know is greater than what is unknown to the people of Madina, and they do not have the same example of the *Salaf* as the people of Madina do.

Another thing is the fact of Madina being a *Haram*. There are multiple hadiths from the Prophet, may Allah bless him and grant him peace, without any defect which affirm that it is a *Haram*. The position of the school of the people of Madina and those who agree with them like ash-Shafi'i and Ibn Hanbal is that it is a *Haram*, but there is disagreement about expiation for killing game there. Those Kufans who disagree with this have not had these *sunan* reach them. Indeed, some of their followers used such hadiths as that of Abu 'Umayr and the hadith of wild animals to bolster their position. Even if these had the same degree of soundness, it still would not be permitted to use them, but in any case the former are multiple transmissions and the hadith of Abu 'Umayr is only taken to apply to game which is caught outside Madina and then brought into it. The same applies to the hadith of wild animals even if it is sound.

And even if the hadiths really are contradictory, it still does not alter the making *haram* of Madina since the hadiths about it being a *Haram* are related by Abu Hurayra and others among those who became Companions later on whereas when the Prophet, may Allah bless him and grant him peace, visited Abu Talha, it was at the beginning of the *hijra*.

Section : Marriage

As for marriages, there is no doubt that the position of the school of the people of Madina is that *muhallil* marriage [a marriage contracted to allow a divorced couple to remarry] and exchange marriage (*shighar*)[1] are both invalid. This is closer to the *Sunna* than the opinion of those people of Iraq who do not consider them invalid. It is affirmed that the Prophet, may Allah bless him and grant him peace, cursed both those who make marriage lawful by means of *muhallil* and also the one whose re-marriage they make lawful, and it is confirmed that the Companions like 'Umar, 'Uthman, 'Ali, Ibn Mas'ud, Ibn 'Umar and Ibn 'Abbas forbade *muhallil* marriage. It is not known that any of them permitted it. This is in accord with the fundamental premises of the people of Madina.

One of their fundamental premises is that intentions must be taken into account when making a contract. They give a prior condition the same status as an accompanying condition and they consider the condition of custom the same as a condition made in words. These fundamental premises cause them to invalidate *muhallil* marriage and also to dismiss any oath which is used merely as a device to enable a person to do what he has sworn to do. On the same basis they also invalidated all devices by which usury is made lawful and all similar things.

Those Kufans who disagree with them regarding that deny the importance of intention in respect of these actions and consider good intention and bad intention to be the same and thus permit actions which have no reality or proper intention, but rather are full of hypocrisy and deceit. As Ayyub as-Sakhtiyati said, "They try to deceive Allah in the way they try to deceive children. If they had done the thing as it should be done it would have been easier for them."

---

1. The *shighar* marriage is one in which one man marries another man's daughter who, in turn, marries his daughter and there is no *mahr* paid by either man.

In his *Sahih* Collection, al-Bukhari relates a chapter on the refutation of the "people of devices". The *Salaf* of the community and their Imams still object to anyone who does that kind of thing as we explained in detail in our book, *al-Mufrad.*

The exchange marriage (*shighar*) was substantiated from the Prophet, may Allah bless him and grant him peace, but not the forbidden form of it. However, those of the Kufans who allow it think that the only questionable thing about it is the fact that the *mahr* is not announced, and that a marriage is still valid without specifying the *mahr.* This is why those who consider it invalid have two approaches.

One approach involves the fact that *shighar* makes consummation in the case of each of the women the *mahr* of the other woman, thus there is an unclear transaction in respect of that consummation, as ash-Shafi'i and many of the people of Ibn Hanbal note. A group of them only consider it invalid when the consummation is actually named as the *mahr* because when it is specified, the transactional element in the consummation vanishes. Some of them only consider it invalid by the actual articulation of the words, "The consummation of each of them is the *mahr* of the other." When that is not said, the consummation is not stipulated as the *mahr.* Some of them invalidate it absolutely as there is an explicit hadith to that effect in the *Sunan* Collections. These three positions exist in the school of Ibn Hanbal and others.

The second approach is that it is invalid by the precondition of the lack of *mahr.* This kind of marriage is one of the special prerogatives of the Prophet, may Allah bless him and grant him peace. According to this, if the *mahr* is specified to be something known to be forbidden, like wine or pork, then the marriage is invalid. That is said by those who say it among the followers of Malik and it is one of the positions in the school of Ahmad ibn Hanbal. It most resembles the clear text of the Qur'an and is closest to analogy based on the fundamental principles.

It is the same in the case of the marriage of a woman who is pregnant or a woman doing *'idda* on account of fornication. That marriage is invalid in the school of Malik, and that is closest to the traditions and analogically best, to ensure that *halal* sperm will not be mixed and confused with the *haram*. Abu Hanifa disagrees with him and permits the contract but not intercourse while ash-Shafi'i allows both.

Ibn Hanbal agrees with them and adds that it is not permitted to marry a fornicatress until she repents as indicated by the Qur'an and the hadiths about the prohibition against marrying a fornicatress. As for those who claim that that is abrogated and that what is meant by that is intercourse [i.e. and not marriage], their statement is clearly incorrect for numerous reasons.

It is the same in the case of a woman who mixes together the *'iddas* from two men, as happens when a woman marries during her *'idda* or has intercourse due to something unclear [i.e. she thinks it is allowed, but it is not]. The school of Malik is that the two *'iddas* do not run concurrently. There is a separate consecutive *'idda* for each of them. This is transmitted from 'Umar and 'Ali, may Allah be pleased with them. It is the school of ash-Shafi'i and Ibn Hanbal. Only Abu Hanifa says that they run concurrently.

Similarly does marriage to a second husband annul less than three pronouncements of divorce? In other words when someone divorces his wife with one or two pronouncements, and then she marries someone who has intercourse with her, and then she returns to her first husband [having divorced the second] does her first husband still have three pronouncements of divorce in hand. According to Malik, she returns to what still remains [i.e. if her first husband divorced her twice, there is only one pronouncement of divorce left, and not three] and this is the position of the great Companions, such as 'Umar ibn al-Khattab and his like. It is also the position of ash-Shafi'i and the best known statement from Ibn Hanbal. Ibn 'Umar and Ibn 'Abbas said that she does not return to what still remains so it as if they start *tabula rasa* and that is the position of Abu Hanifa.

It is the same with the *ila'*.[1] The school of the people of Madina and the *fuqaha'* of hadith and others is that there is a respite at the end of four months, and a man can either take his wife back or divorce her. This is what is transmitted from about ten of the Companions. The Qur'an and the sources also clearly indicate this. The position of the Kufans is that divorce is obliged at the end of the period. When it ends and he has not taken her back, then she is automatically divorced.

There is also the question of a man returning to his wife [after a non-final divorce] by action, as when he has intercourse with her. Does intercourse constitute a legal return to marriage? There are three positions. One is that it does constitute that, as Abu Hanifa says. The second is that it does not, as ash-Shafi'i says. The third is that it does amount to a return when that is the intention in it, and that is the famous position of Malik, and it is the most just of the three positions in the school of Ahmad ibn Hanbal.

---

1. A type of divorce in which a man vows not to have intercourse with his wife. If it lasts for four months, then the divorce takes place.

Section: Judgements and Punishments

As for punishments and judgements, the school of the people of Madina is preferred to the school of the people of Kufa in various ways.

One of them is that they require retaliation in case of killing to be by a similar method to that of the original act, which is what the *Sunna* came with, and as the fundamental principles in fact indicate. Indeed, Malik went so far as to deny that accidental killing is like intentional killing at all, although others disagreed with him concerning that, since it ignores the resemblance that is there. In reality, however, it [i.e. intentional killing,] is a type of error which is distinguished by a much harsher judgement, and indeed this is mentioned in the Qur'an.

Another question is whether a Muslim is killed in retaliation for a *kafir* or *dhimmi*, and a free man for a slave. People take three positions regarding this matter. One is that a Muslim is killed for his victim in every case, which is the position of Abu Hanifa and his people. The second is that he is not killed for him in any case, as is the position of ash-Shafi'i and one of the two positions of Ibn Hanbal. The third is that he is not killed for him except in the case of brigandage (*muhâraba*). Killing in that case is a *hadd* punishment for the sake of the general public welfare and equivalence[1] is not necessary in it. Indeed, in such a case a freeman is killed even if the murdered man is a slave, and a Muslim is killed even if the murdered man was a *dhimmi*. This is the position of the people of Madina and the second position of Ibn Hanbal. It is the most just of the positions and regarding it the transmitted traditions about this subject are also in agreement.

The position of Malik regarding brigands and others is to carry out judgement on both accessories to the act and those directly involved, the same as is generally agreed in judgements concerning *jihad*. Those who disagree with this position concede

---

1. i.e. Muslim for Muslim, free man for free man, etc.

that there must be retaliation against those who took any part in the killing. It is agreed upon by all the Imams going by the words of 'Umar: "If all the people of Sana' had abetted it, I would have killed them for it."

If they were all directly involved, there is no dispute. If some of them were not directly involved, but merely part of the general cause which led to killing, such as people forced to take part, or false witnesses who retract their testimony, or unjust judges who withdraw their judgement, then most people make them accountable and retaliation is obliged against such people. That is as 'Ali said about the two men who testified that a man had stolen, causing his hand to be cut off, and then they retracted their evidence saying, "We erred." He said, "If I thought that you had done it deliberately, I would have cut your hands off." This indicates the cutting off of hands in return for cutting off hands and the obligation of retaliation in the case of false witnessing.

The Kufans disagree about these two cases. 'Umar ibn al-Khattab, may Allah be pleased with him, considered all the brigands as a single entity [i.e. acting as one person] and it is known that the position of those who consider that those who aid and abet in wrong action and aggression should share in the punishment is more in conformity with the Book and the *Sunna* in both letter and spirit than the position of those who only advocate punishment for the person directly involved.

❋❋❋❋❋

Another thing is that the people of Madina follow what 'Umar ibn al-Khattab said on the *minbar* of the Messenger of Allah, may Allah bless him and grant him peace, when he stated, "Stoning in the Book of Allah is a duty to be inflicted on men and women who fornicate when they are *muhsan* and the proof is established or there is pregnancy or confession." That is also their position when carrying out the *hadd* in respect of wine when someone is found drunk or vomiting from it or it is smelt on him and there is no uncertainty involved. This is what is related from the Prophet, may Allah bless him and grant him peace, and his Rightly-guided Khalifs, like 'Umar, 'Uthman and 'Ali.

Abu Hanifa and ash-Shafi'i do not think that a *hadd* punishment should be applied except when there is confession or clear proof of the action. They claim that that is because of doubt. Both transmissions come from Ahmad ibn Hanbal.

It is known that the first position is more like the *Sunna* of the Messenger of Allah, may Allah bless him and grant him peace, and the *Sunna* of his Rightly-guided Khalifs. It is preserving the limits of Allah Almighty which Allah Almighty commanded to be preserved. Doubt in this matter is like doubt in the proof and confession which can be lies or error.

Another thing is that the people of Madina think that penalties in respect of property are prescribed when they are from the *Sunna* of the Messenger of Allah, may Allah bless him and grant him peace, and the *Sunna* of his Rightly-Guided khalifs, just as physical penalties are prescribed when they are from the *Sunna*. Penalties in respect of property are denied by several of the people of Kufa and those who follow them. They claim that they were abrogated. From where do they adduce proof of their abrogation? They often do this even when they see a sound hadith opposing their position. As for the scholars of the people of Madina and the scholars of hadith, they think that the *sunan* and traditions contain penalties in respect of property just as they contain physical penalties, such as breaking wine jugs and splitting wine-skins and burning wine taverns.

That is what Musa did in the case of the Calf (20:97) and the Prophet, may Allah bless him and grant him peace, did with idols [inside the Ka'ba], and when he commanded 'Abdullah ibn 'Amr to burn two saffron garments, and when he first commanded the pots containing donkey-meat to be broken and subsequently permitted that they be washed. In the hadith reported by 'Abdullah ibn 'Umar ibn al-Khattab, a fine was imposed in the case of the lost camel which was in fact concealed. The blood-money of a *dhimmi* who had been killed deliberately was also doubled.

It is the same with regard to their position generally in respect of retaliation and blood money – it is the soundest of positions. One aspect of it is the blood money of *dhimmis*. Some people say their blood money is the same as that of Muslims, and this is the position of Abu Hanifa, and some of them say that their blood money is a third of that of a Muslim because it is the least possible amount as ash-Shafi'i states. The third position is that their blood money is half of that of a Muslim, and this is the position of Malik, and it is the soundest of positions because this is transmitted from the Prophet, may Allah bless him and grant him peace, as the compilers of the *Sunan* collections, Abu Dawud and others, relate from the Prophet, may Allah bless him and grant him peace.

Another aspect of this matter is whether relatives are responsible for paying all blood money, as ash-Shafi'i says, or are merely responsible for certain amounts of blood money such as the blood money for head wounds which bare the bone and for the loss of fingers and more serious injuries than those, as Abu Hanifa says, or are only liable for any amount over one third of the full blood money, which is the position of Malik. This is what is transmitted, and it is the position of Ibn Hanbal. There are two statements regarding this third in the school of Malik and Ibn Hanbal.

It is said that a Madinan and a Kufan were arguing and the Madinan said to the Kufan, "You are blessed in the quarter. According to you it is only necessary to wipe a quarter of the head and you overlook an impurity which covers less than a quarter of the place and you say the same in respect of other things."

The Kufan said, "And you are blessed in the third since, according to you, a third is sufficient for one who has vowed to give away his property as *sadaqa*, and relatives are only responsible for paying any amount which is over a third of the full blood money, and the blood-money for injuries done to a woman is the same as that of a man as long as it does not exceed a third of the full blood money. If it is does, she gets half of what a man gets. And there are other similar instances."

This is sound, but nevertheless it must be said to the Kufan, "There is no basis for the quarter either in the Book of Allah nor the *Sunna* of His Messenger." The Kufans reply, "Man has four sides, and you say, 'I saw a man' when you only saw one side of him. So a man consists of four sides, and the quarter is in the same position as the whole."

As for the third, it has a basis elsewhere in the *Sunna* of the Messenger of Allah, may Allah bless him and grant him peace. It is established by the sound *Sunna* and the agreement of the Muslims that a sick person can will away a third of his property and no more, as the Prophet, may Allah bless him and grant him peace, instructed Sa'd ibn Abi Waqqas when he visited him in the Farewell Hajj. It is established in the *Sahih* Collection in the case of the man who freed six slaves of his when he died, that the Prophet divided them into three: he freed two, and left four as slaves. It is related that he said to Abu Lubaba, "A third is enough for you," and it is in other places. So where is the Kufan position in relation to all this? But the Madinan position is backed up by these hadiths .

Drawing lots

Drawing lots is the subject of an *ayat* in the Book of Allah and there are six *hadiths* about it from the Prophet, peace be upon him, including the following:

"If people had known what was in the call to prayer and the first row, they would have found no other way except to draw lots for it."

It is known that when the Prophet wanted to travel, he drew lots between his wives, and whichever of them had her lot come out went out with him. The Ansar drew lots for the Muhajirun when they emigrated to them. There were also two claimants whom the Prophet commanded to draws lots having taken an oath to accept the result, like it or not. Another example was the two people who argued about an inheritance which was unclear and he said to them, "Try to reach the truth and draw lots so that each of you make his brother's position lawful."

The drawing of lots which the people of Madina and those who agree with them like ash-Shafi'i, Ibn Hanbal and others allow, is disallowed by the Kufans who do not permit it. It is transmitted that one of them said, "Drawing lots is gambling." They made it part of gambling, but the difference between the lot-drawing which the Messenger of Allah, may Allah bless him and grant him peace, prescribed as *sunna*, and the gambling which he forbade, is clear and evident. Drawing lots takes place when the rights are equal and it is not possible to single out one. This falls into two categories.

One of them is in the case where the one who deserves it is not specified, like two partners when the thing to be divided is absent, in which case it is allotted to one of them by drawing lots, and like the slaves whom the Prophet divided into three, and like the wives when he wanted to travel with one of them. There is no disagreement about this and both positions say that lots are drawn in such a case.

The second category is that the one specified does not intrinsically deserve it, as in the case of the story of the Prophet Yunus and those who challenged each other [i.e. by drawing lots to see who would be thrown overboard], or like the lots in the case when someone has freed a slave and then forgotten which one it was, or the instance where a man divorced one of his wives and then forgot which one it was and then dies or similar instances. These are cases where lots are used in which there is dispute and Ibn Hanbal permits that but ash-Shafi'i does not.

Section: Judgement in Claims

Their position in respect of judgements is that they prefer the stronger of the two claimants and give him the benefit of the oath and in cases where rights are in dispute they give judgement on the basis of one witness and the oath of the plaintiff. In the *qasama*[1] they begin with the oath of the plaintiffs. If they swear fifty oaths, then they have the right to blood. The Kufans think that only the person against whom the claim is made should swear and they do not make the plaintiff swear in the *qasama* or any other instance nor do they give judgement on the basis of one witness and an oath and they do not think that a plaintiff has to take any oath.

It is known that the sound *Sunna* of the Prophet, may Allah bless him and grant him peace, accords with the position of the Madinans. The hadith regarding the *qasama* is sound and confirmed. The Prophet told the Ansar, "Let fifty take oaths and then you have the right to the blood of your companion." When ash-Shafi'i and his like among the people of Iraq argued with the scholars of the people of Madina like Abu'z-Zinad and others about the *qasama*, and the people of Madina used the *Sunna* as a proof to which no one can fail to submit, the Madinans said to them, "The *Sunna* and the principles of truth accord something which differs from reasoned opinion, and so the Muslims must accept it" in a long discussion which is transmitted by *isnad*.

It is the same with the question of giving judgement on the basis of one witness and an oath. There are hadiths about this in the *Sahih* and *Sunan* Collections, like the hadith of Ibn 'Abbas which Muslim related and the *hadith* of Abu Hurayra and others which is related by Abu Dawud. When some of the scholars said, "We think that one witness and an oath is invalid," scholars like Malik, ash-Shafi'i, Ahmad ibn Hanbal, Abu 'Ubayd and others

---

1. An oath taken by fifty members of a tribe or locality to refute accusations of complicity in unclear murder cases. Or when the relatives of a murder victim swear to the guilt of an individual. Such a case might rise when the victim named his murderer before dying and his relatives swear to that.

support this *sunna*. Malik advocates it in his *Muwatta'* in a way unequalled in any other instance in the *Muwatta'*, as does ash-Shafi'i in the *Umm* where he devotes about ten pages to it. Abu 'Ubayd does the same in the *Book of Judgement*.

The Kufans only have what they relate that the Prophet said: "The clear proof is on the claimant and the oath is taken by the defendant." This sentence is not in the *Sunan*.[1] Some of the authors related it among the hadiths, but the *Sahih* contains the hadith of Ibn 'Abbas that the Prophet, may Allah bless him and grant him peace, said, "If people were to be given according to their claims, some people would claim the blood and property of other people, but the oath is taken by the one against whom the claim is made."

If it is said that this expression is not general, the *lam* is the definite article[2] for the one against whom the claim is made since the plaintiff has nothing except his claim as he said, "If people were to be given according to their claims..." Those who make the plaintiff swear, do not do so only on the basis of the claim itself. Rather they make him swear when the proof is established which gives his side the ascendancy, as in the case of the witness in rights and inheritance in the *qasama*.

Their taking as evidence the *ayats* in the Qur'an which mention two witnesses, and one man and two women, is very weak indeed. When this is mentioned, it is a question of testimony, not of giving judgement. If it had been about judgement, then in that case judgement could be given on the basis of testimony alone and no oath would be needed. If anyone does insist on an oath in addition to one witness, then he is, in any case, giving judgement on the basis of testimony different to what is mentioned in the Qur'an.

All the Imams also agree that judgement can be given without any testimony at all. In fact it can be based on the refusal to testi-

1. Ibn Taymiyya is mistaken here. Al-Bukhari and Muslim have *hadiths* with different wording, but with the same implication.
2. This is grammatical. The *lam li-ta'rif al-ma'hud* is an article used to indicate something already mentioned

fy or make denial. Judgement can also be given on the basis of the testimony of individual women in certain instances. How could judgement be given unless this was not contrary to the Qur'an?

Then Malik made retaliation mandatory on the basis of *qasama* and carried out the *hadd* on the woman when the man took the oath and the woman did not. Ash-Shafi'i carries out the *hadd* and but does not kill on the basis of *qasama*. Abu Hanifa takes a different position in both instances. Ibn Hanbal agrees with the retaliation on the basis of *qasama* but not the *hadd* of the woman. He imprisons her when she refuses to take the oath and dissolves her marriage. The literal meaning of the Book and the *Sunna* confirms the position of Malik.

❋❋❋❋❋

Another position held by the people of Madina is that sodomites are put to death – both the passive and active partners, whether they are *muhsan* or not. This is what the *Sunna* indicates and it tallies with what the Companions said. It is one of two positions in the schools of ash-Shafi'i and Ibn Hanbal. Those of the Kufans who say that they should not be killed have neither the *Sunna* nor any tradition from the Companions to support their position. Rabi' said to the Kufan who disputed this, "Would you make something that is not lawful in any case the same as something that is allowed in one case and not in another?" Az-Zuhri mentioned that killing was the *Sunna*.

Another thing is allegation in cases such as theft and murder. In such a case they examine the circumstances of the suspect. Is the allegation really justified or not? They think that there is punishment for someone against whom suspicion appears justified. That is mentioned by the author of *The Judgements of the Sultan* (*Al-Ahkam as-Sultaniyya*)[1] from the people of ash-Shafi'i and from Ahmad ibn Hanbal. They mentioned the punishment

---

1. Al-Mawardi.

of such people and whether the ruler and *qadi* should punish him or not punish him. There are two positions. In view of the fact that it is obligatory to recognise that the authority of Allah Almighty and His Messenger is transferred to each person who judges between people, whether he be a ruler, a judge or whatever, the first position is that anyone who makes a distinction between this area of allegation and that which is connected to the explicit commands of Allah and His Messenger has erred. The second position is when someone makes a distinction between the two of them in respect of whether the matter in question is related to governance or the judiciary since a ruler has authority over things like that whereas a judge does not.

In several speeches and books some of the followers of the Kufans support their position by the cases of those whom the Prophet, may Allah bless him and grant him peace, killed or commanded to be killed, like the Jew who had crushed a girl's head, and the captive he took although she had a treaty, and sodomites and other similar cases. They claim that he only did this out of policy!

It is said to them: if you say that this policy is prescribed for us, then it is true and it is prescribed policy in the *Shari'a*. If you say that it is not prescribed for us, then this entails opposition to the *Sunna*. The position is either that people should adopt this policy as part of the *Shari'a* of Islam or that this policy is not part of the *Shari'a* of Islam. If the first is said, then it is clearly part of the *deen*. If the second is said, then it is an error.

However, the real source of this error is that the school of the Kufans is lacking in knowledge of the policy of the Messenger of Allah, may Allah bless him and grant him peace, and the policy of his Rightly-guided Khalifs. It is affirmed in the *Sahih* Collections that the Prophet said, "The tribe of Israel used to give leadership to their Prophets. Whenever a Prophet died, another Prophet arose. There is no Prophet after me, but there will be many khalifs." They said, "What do you command us to do?" He said, "Fulfil allegiance to the first and then the next and give

86

them their rights, Allah will question them about that which was in their care."

When the khalifate went to the Abbasids and they needed to manage the people and to appoint judges for them from the *fuqaha'* of Iraq, they did not have adequate knowledge of policy. At that time they needed to establish a post dealing with injustices and another dealing with war, which are not prescribed posts, and these things spread rapidly through many of the Muslim cities until people began to talk about "the *Shari'a* and policy" as separate entities. This one calls his opponent to the *Shari'a* and that one calls him to policy. This allowed one ruler to rule by the *Shari'a* and another to rule by policy.

The reason for that is that those who claim to judge by the *Shari'a* are in fact lacking in knowledge of the *Sunna*. So when they give judgement in many matters, they deprive people of their rights and fail to observe the limits to the extent that they shed blood without right and usurp people's property and make unlawful things lawful. Those who judge by the dictates of policy begin to rule by mere opinion without any reliance on the Book and the *Sunna*, and the best of them are those who rule without bias and seek justice. Many of them rule with bias, loving the strong and those who bribe them, and other such people.

The case with the cities in which the school of the people of Madina predominated was that there was judgement with justice in them, something which was not the case in other cities. Those who consider the people who are fought to be in the same category as the people of the Book with regard to property are people of the cities in which the school of the people of Iraq and those who follow them predominates since, in these cities, the minister of war does not follow the people of knowledge.

Allah Almighty says in His Book, *"We sent Our Messengers with the Clear Signs and We sent down the Book and the Balance with them ..."* (57:25) So the governance of the *deen* is guided by the Book and given victory by the sword. *"Your Lord is a sufficient guide and helper."* (25:31) The *deen* of Islam is that the sword follows the

Book. When knowledge of the Book and *Sunna* has the upper hand, and the sword follows it, then the business of Islam is established. The people of Madina are nearer to this than those of any other city. In the time of the Rightly-guided Khalifs, that was the way it was. After them, sometimes the situation varied. When knowledge of the Book is insufficient and the sword sometimes agrees with the Book and sometimes opposes it, then where is the *deen* to be found in that?

Whoever is guided in all these matters and others like them will see clearly that the basic premises of the people of Madina are incomparably sounder than those of any other people on the earth. There is no comparison between them.

✳✳✳✳✳

Another thing is the fighting in the Great *Fitna* (Civil War). The Companions formed into three groups in it. There was one group who fought on one side, another group who fought on the other side, and a third group who took no part in it. The *fuqaha'* today have two positions. Some of them think that fighting on the side of 'Ali was correct, in other words fighting rebels, and some think that the correct position was to take no part, and that is the well-known position of the people of Madina and the people of hadith. The sound firm hadiths from the Prophet, may Allah bless him and grant him peace, on the subject of this *fitna* agree with the position of those people. This is why the authors of the *'aqida* formulations of the people of the *Sunna* and the Community as a whole mention not fighting in the way of *fitna* and are the most reticent about what occurred between the Companions.

✳✳✳✳✳

The people of Madina, however, believe in fighting anyone who goes out of the *Shari'a*, such as the Haruriyya and others, and they make a distinction between this and fighting in the way of *fitna*. This is also the position of the *fuqaha'* of hadith and it is what tallies with the *Sunna* of the Messenger of Allah, may Allah bless him and grant him peace, and the *Sunna* of his Rightly-guided Khalifs. The hadith about the Kharijites is confirmed from the Prophet. Muslim transmitted it in his *Sahih* Collection and al-Bukhari transmitted some of it. He said in it, "You should disdain to pray behind them, fast with their fast or recite with their recitation. They recite the Qur'an but it does not pass beyond their throats. They pass through Islam as an arrow passes through game. Fight them wherever you find them. There will be a reward with Allah on the Day of Rising for anyone who kills them."

The agreement of the Companions to fight them is confirmed and the *Amir al-Mu'minin* 'Ali, may Allah be pleased with him, fought them. He mentioned the *Sunna* of the Messenger of Allah, may Allah bless him and grant him peace, in respect of them which included fighting them, and he delighted in killing them and prostrated to Allah out of thankfulness when he saw Dhu'th-Thudayya[1] killed, which is very different to the way he behaved at the Battle of the Camel and at the Battle of Siffin.[2] 'Ali was not happy then. Indeed pain and regret showed in him. He did not mention a *sunna* from the Messenger of Allah in respect of that. Rather he mentioned that he was fighting on those occasions by his own *ijtihad*.

The people of Madina followed the *Sunna* in fighting everyone who left the *Shari'a* but they did not fight in the *fitna*, which was also the position of the people of hadith in contradistinction to those who considered fighting these and those to be the same.

---

1. The leader of the Kharijites in the Battle of Nahrawan in 38/658. The hadith mentioned that there would be someone with a deformed arm among them and Dhu'th-Thudayya had such a defect. 'Ali was pleased because it proved that he had been correct in his decision to fight them.

2. The Battle of the Camel was one of the major incidents of the first Civil War (*Fitna*) in which the forces of 'Ali defeated the forces of 'A'isha, Talha, and az-Zubayr in a battle fought outside Basra in 36/656. Siffin is a location in Syria where, in 38/657, a battle between 'Ali and Mu'awiya took place.

Indeed, they considered fighting the former the same as when Abu Bakr as-Siddiq fought those who refused to pay *zakat*. People who consider the people of *fitna* the same as rebels join together what Allah has made separate but the people of Madina and the *Sunna* consider as separate what Allah has made separate and follow the sound text and just straight analogy. Sound analogy is part of justice. It is to make two things which are alike equal and to distinguish between two things which are different. The people of Madina are the people who most followed the sound text and just analogy.

✳✳✳✳✳

This subject is too long to deal with fully. However hopefully we have pointed out some of the things by which the virtues of the people of the City of the Prophet will be known and recognised. Knowledge of this matter is part of the *deen*, especially when people are ignorant of the value of their knowledge and *deen*. So making this clear is as important as making the knowledge of the Companions and their *deen* clear when someone is ignorant of that.

In the same way that the clarification of the *Sunna* and the virtues of the Companions and their advancement of Abu Bakr as-Siddiq and 'Umar al-Faruq is the greatest support of the *deen* in the face of the appearance of the innovations of the Rafidites and their like, so also the clarification of the *Sunna* and the school of the people of Madina and its superiority over all the schools of the other cities of Islam is the greatest support of the *deen* in the face of the appearance of the innovations of the ignorant who follow their own opinions and desires. And Allah knows best.

May Allah Almighty give success to us and all our believing brothers in what He loves and pleases Him. Praise be to Allah, Lord of the worlds, and may Allah bless Sayyiduna Muhammad and his family and Companions and grant them peace.

Glossary

Abbasids: the dynasty of khalifs who ruled from 132/750 to 656/1258 and had their capital in Baghdad. They based their claim to power on their descent from al-'Abbas, the uncle of the Prophet.

abdan: the plural of *badan*, "body", used in *sharika al-abdan*, partnership in physical labour for gain.

adhan: the call to prayer.

'amal: action, normative practice, precedent, juridical practice.

Amir al-Mu'minin: "the Commander of the Believers," the khalif.

Ansar: the "Helpers", the people of Madina who welcomed and aided the Prophet.

'aqida: creed, belief or tenet of faith firmly based on how things are, distinct from the testimony of faith (*shahada*).

'ariyya: a kind of sale by which the owner of the fruit of one or more palms is allowed to sell the fresh dates while they are still on the palms by means of estimation, for dried plucked dates.

'Asr: the mid-afternoon prayer.

ayat: a verse of the Qur'an.

basmala: the Arabic expression, "In the Name of Allah, the All-Merciful, All-Compassionate."

Dajjal: the false Messiah whose appearance marks the imminent end of the world.

deen: the life-transaction, lit. the debt between two parties, in this usage between the Creator and created.

dhimma: obligation or contract, in particular a treaty of protection for non-Muslims living in Muslim territory.

dhimmi: a non-Muslim living under the protection of Muslim rule.

Dhuhr: the midday prayer.

Fajr: the two *rak'at* prayer at dawn performed before the obligatory prayer of *Subh*.

faqih: a man learned in knowledge of *fiqh* (see below) who by virtue of his knowledge can give a legal judgement.

fatwa: an authoritative statement on a point of law.

fiqh: the science of the application of the *Shari'a*. A practitioner or expert in *fiqh* is called a *faqih* (see above).

Fitna: civil strife, sedition, schism, trial, temptation. The Great Fitna took place after the murder of 'Uthman.

fuqaha': the plural of *faqih* (see above).

habal al-habala: a forbidden business transaction in which a man buys the unborn offspring of a female animal.

ghusl: full ritual bath.

habous: a *waqf* (see below).

hadath: minor ritual impurity requiring *wudu'*: passing wind, urination, defecation, vomiting.

hadd: Allah's boundary limits for the lawful and unlawful. The *hadd* punishments are specific fixed penalties laid down by Allah for specified crimes.

hadith: reported speech of the Prophet.

hajj: the annual pilgrimage to Makka which is one of the five pillars of Islam.

halal: lawful according to the *Shari'a*.

Haram: Sacred Precinct, a protected area in which certain behaviour is forbidden and other behaviour necessary. The area around the Ka'ba in Makka is a Haram, and the area around the Prophet's Mosque in Madina is a Haram. They are referred to together as al-Haramayn, 'the two Harams'.

haram: unlawful according to the *Shari'a*.

Haruriyya: A term used to denote the early Kharijites, from the name of the village which was their centre.

Hijaz: the region along the western seaboard of Arabia in which Makka, Madina, Jeddah and Ta'if are situated.

Hijra: emigration in the way of Allah. Islamic dating begins with the *Hijra* of the Prophet Muhammad from Makka to Madina in 622 AD.

hiyal: legal devices, evasions, observing the letter, but not the spirit of the law.

'id: a festival, either the festival at the end of Ramadan or at the time of the *Hajj*.

'idda: a period after divorce or the death of her husband for which a woman must wait before re-marrying.

ihram: the conditions of clothing and behaviour adopted by someone on hajj or 'umra.

ijtihad: to exercise personal judgement in legal matters.

ila': a vow by a husband to abstain from sexual relations with his wife. If four months pass, it is considered a divorce.

'inan: in Maliki law, a partnership limited to either a single commodity or a single transaction. For Malikis, Hanbalis and Hanafis contributions cannot be credit, and for Shafi'is they cannot be chattels or labour. It implies mutual agency but not mutual surety with regard to the work undertaken and salary owed to employees.

'Isha': the night prayer.

isnad: a tradition's chain of transmission from individual to individual.

i'tikaf: seclusion, while fasting, in a mosque, particularly in the last ten days of Ramadan.

Jahiliyya: the Time of Ignorance before the coming of Islam.

Jahmiyya: followers of Jahm ibn Safwan (d. 128/745) who taught that Allah has no attributes and that man has no free will of any sort at all.

jamra: lit. a small walled place, but in this usage a stone-built pillar. There are three *jamras* at Mina. One of the rites of *hajj* is to stone them.

janaba: major ritual impurity requiring a *ghusl*: incurred by intercourse, sexual discharge, menstruation, childbirth.

Jibril: the angel Gabriel who brought the revelation of the Qur'an to the Prophet Muhammad, may Allah bless him and grant him peace.

jihad: struggle, particularly fighting in the way of Allah to establish Islam.

Jumu'a: the day of gathering, Friday, and particularly the *Jumu'a* prayer which is performed instead of *Dhuhr* on Friday by those who attend it.

junub: being in a state of *janaba*. (See above.)

kafir: a person who rejects Allah and His Messenger. The opposite is believer or *mu'min*.

Kharijites: the earliest sect, who separated themselves from the body of the Muslims and declared war on all those who disagreed with them, stating that a wrong action turns a Muslim into an unbeliever.

Khaybar: a Jewish colony to the north of Madina which was laid siege to and captured by the Muslims in the seventh year after the Hijra because of the Jews' continual treachery.

Khorasan: Persian province southeast of the Caspian Sea; a centre of many dissident movements in early Islamic history.

Maghrib: the sunset prayer; the western part of Muslim lands. Today it means Morocco.

mahr: dower given by a husband to his wife on marriage.

Mihna: the Inquisition instituted by the Abbasid khalif, al-Ma'mun, which required all important people to state publicly that they believed that the Qur'an was created, not uncreated.

miqat: one of the designated places for entering into *ihram* for *'umra* or *hajj.*

mithqal: the weight of one dinar, the equivalent of 72 grains of barley (equals 4.4 grams). It may be somewhat less or more. [10 dirhams weigh 7 *mithqals.*]

mudâraba: commenda, co-partnership, *qirad.*

mudd: a measure of volume, approximately a double-handed scoop.

Muhajirun: Companions of the Messenger of Allah who accepted Islam in Makka and made *hijra* to Madina.

muhallil: a man who marries a woman who has been trebly divorced on the condition that he then divorce her in order that her first husband can remarry her. Marriage solely for this purpose is not permitted.

muhaqala: a forbidden sale in which, for instance, unharvested wheat was bartered for harvested wheat, or land was rented for wheat, or wheat for seeds.

muhsan: (or *muhsin*) a person who has been married.

mulamasa: a forbidden sale, in which the deal is completed if the buyer touches a thing without seeing or checking it properly.

munabadha: a forbidden sale in which the deal is completed when the seller throws things towards the buyer without giving him a chance to see, touch or check them.

Murji'ites: the opponents of the Kharijites. They held that it is faith and not actions which are important. There is also a political position which suspends judgement on a person guilty of major sins.

mursal: a hadith where a man in the generation after the Companions quotes directly from the Prophet without mentioning the Companion from whom he got it.

musâqa: sharecropping contract; tending to an existing plantation in exchange for a share of the yield.

mutakallim: someone who studies the science of *kalam*, the science of investigating theological doctrine.

mutawâtir: a hadith which is reported by a large number of reporters at all stages of the *isnad* (see above).

Mu'tazilites: someone who adheres to the school of the Mu'tazila which is rationalist in its approach to existence. Originally they held that anyone who commits a sin is neither a believer nor an unbeliever. They also held the Qur'an to be created.

muzabana: a forbidden sale in which something whose number, weight, or measure is known is sold for something whose number, weight or measure is not known.

muzâra'a: farming partnership, in which someone allows his land to be cultivated in exchange for a portion of the produce.

nabidh: a drink made by soaking grapes, raisins, dates, etc, in water without allowing them to ferment to the point of becoming intoxicating. If it does become intoxicating, it is still called *nabidh.*

Nasibiyya: a group of people who dislike 'Ali and his family; they are the counterpart of the Rafidites.

nisab: minimum amount of wealth on which *zakat* must be paid.

Qadariyya: sect who said that people have power (*qadar*) over their actions and hence free will.

qadi: a judge, qualified to judge all matters in accordance with the *Shari'a* and to dispense and enforce legal punishments.

qasama: an oath taken by fifty members of a tribe or locality to refute or establish accusations of complicity in unclear cases of homicide.

qiran: performing *hajj* and *'umra* simultaneously.

qirad: wealth put by an investor in the trust of an agent for use for commercial purposes, the agent receiving no wage, but taking a designated share of the profits after the capital has been repaid.

Rafidites: group of the Shi'a known for rejecting Abu Bakr and 'Umar as well as 'Uthman.

rak'at: a unit of the prayer consisting of a series of standings, bowing, prostrations and sittings.

ra'y: opinion, personal discretion.

riba: usury, which is unlawful whatever forms it takes, since it it involves obtaining something for nothing through exploitation.

riba al-fadl: this involves any discrepancy in quantity in an exchange, for example, an exchange of goods of superior quality for more of the same kind of goods of inferior quality, e.g., dates of superior quality for dates of inferior quality in greater amount. This is forbidden.

riba an-nasi'a: this involves a gap in time in an exchange of two quantities, even if they match in quantity and quality, for instance, interest on lent money.

ritl: a measure of weight, approximately one pound.

ruku': the bowing position in the prayer.

sa': a measure of volume equal to four *mudds*.

sa'y: the main rite of *'umra* and part of *hajj*. It is going between the hills of Safa and Marwa seven times.

Sahih: "the Sound", the title of the hadith collections of al-Bukhari and Muslim.

Salaf: the early generations of the Muslims.

salam: the expression, *"as-salamu 'alaykum,"* or "Peace be upon you," used as a greeting and to end the prayer.

shaf': lit. "even", a supererogatory prayer performed with the *witr* (see below).

Shari'a: the legal modality of a people based on the revelation of their Prophet. The final *Shari'a* is that of Islam.

shighar: a forbidden form of marriage agreement whereby a man gave his daughter in marriage to another man who in return gave his daughter in marriage to him, without either of them paying any *mahr* to their respective brides.

sunan: plural of *sunna*.

Sunan: collections of hadiths which concentrate on legal rulings, like Abu Dawud, an-Nasa'i and others.

Sunna: the customary practice of a person or group of people. It has come to refer almost exclusively to the practice of the Messenger of Allah, may Allah bless him and grant him peace.

Tabi'un: the second generation of the early Muslims who did not meet the Prophet Muhammad, may Allah bless him and grant him peace, but learned the *deen* of Islam from his Companions.

tafsir: commentary of explanation of the meanings of the Qur'an.

takbir: saying *"Allahu Akbar,"* "Allah is greater".

takbir al-ihram: the *takbir* which begins the prayer.

talbiya: saying *"Labbayk"* ("At Your service") during the *hajj*.

taqlid: imitation; following the opinion of a *mujtahid* without considering the evidence.

tawaf: circumambulation of the Ka'ba, done in sets of seven circuits.

tawaf al-ifada: the *tawaf* of the Ka'ba that the pilgrims must perform after coming from Mina to Makka on the 10th of Dhu'l-Hijja. It is one of the essential rites of *hajj*.

tawâtur: the quality of being *mutawatir* (see above).

tayammum; purification for the prayer with clean dust, earth, or stone, when water for *ghusl* or *wudu'* is unavailable or would be detrimental to health.

Umayyads: the Muslim dynasty of khalifs who ruled in Damascus from 40/661 onwards until they were overthrown by the Abbasids in 132/750.

'umra: the lesser pilgrimage to the Ka'ba in Makka performed at any time of the year.

'ushr: one tenth of the yield of land.

waqf: also *habous*, an unalienable endowment for a charitable purpose which cannot be given away or sold to anyone.

wasq: a measure of volume equal to sixty *sa's*.

witr: lit. "odd", a single *rak'at* prayed immediately after the *shaf* after the night prayer which makes the number of *sunna* prayers uneven.

wudu': ritual washing to be pure for the prayer.

zakat: a wealth tax, one of the five pillars of Islam.

Biographical Notes

'**Abdullah ibn 'Abdu'l-Hakam:** a (d. 214/830), a Shafi'i scholar in Egypt.

'**Abdullah ibn 'Amr ibn al-'As:** : (d. 65/684), a Companion. It is said that he transmitted even more from the Prophet than Abu Hurayra did but few people came to see him in Egypt.

'**Abdullah ibn Mas'ud:** *see Ibn Mas'ud.*

'**Abdullah ibn al-Mubarak:** a famous scholar from Marv who was born in 118/736. He was an ascetic man with knowledge of hadith, *fiqh*, literature, grammar, language, and poetry. He wrote several books and was the first to produce a book on *jihad*. He died in Hit, Iraq, in 181/797 after a battle with the Byzantines.

'**Abdullah ibn Rawaha:** al-Ansari, the poet of the Prophet and his third general, after Zayd ibn Haritha and Ja'far ibn Abi Talib, in the expedition to Mu'ta where he was killed along with the other two. He died in 8/629.

'**Abdullah ibn Wahb:** *see Ibn Wahb.*

'**Abdu'l-'Aziz ibn Abi Salama al-Majishun:** *see Ibn al-Majishun.*

'**Abdu'r-Rahman ibn Mahdi:** *see Ibn Mahdi.*

'**Abdu'l-Wahhab ibn 'Ali:** (362/973-422/1031), a Maliki *faqih* in Baghdad at the beginning of the eleventh century, author of *Ishraf*, *qadi* over 'Askar al-Mahdi (Rusafa) and then moved to Egypt.

Abu Ayyub al-Ansari: Khalid ibn Zayd: one of the Banu'n-Najjar. He was present at 'Aqaba, Badr, Uhud, the Ditch and all the battles. He fell ill, died and was buried at the base of the fortifications of Constantinople in 52/672.

Abu Bakr as-Siddiq: (d. 13/634), a Makkan merchant who was three years younger than the Prophet and was the Prophet's closest Companion. He became the first Khalif after the death of the Prophet.

Abu'd-Darda': (d. 32/652), a Companion.

Abu Dawud as-Sijistani: (203/817-275-888) the author of the *Sunan*, one of the six canonical volumes of hadith. He was one of the greatest of the scholars of hadith.

Abu Hanifa: (d. 150/767), founder of the Hanafi school, one of the four Imams, a *faqih* and *mujtahid*. He was a hadith expert who had all the hadiths of Makka and Madina in addition to those of Kufa. He developed *ra'y* (legal opinion).

Abu Hurayra: (d. c. 58/677-8) a Companion who is one of the most prolific narrators of hadiths. He became Muslim after the Khaybar expedition (7/629) and was one of the *Ahl as-Suffa*. He acted as governor of Bahrayn under 'Umar.

Abu Ja'far al-Mansur: *see al-Mansur.*

Abu Lubaba: a Companion who died in Madina while 'Ali was khalif.

Abu Sa'id al-Khudri: Sa'id ibn Malik ibn Sinan, a Companion of high rank, one of the Ansar of Khazraj, famous among the *fuqaha'* of the Companions who took part in 12 battles with the Prophet and died in Madina and was buried in al-Baqi' in 74/694. Many hadiths are related from him.

Abu Thawr: (d. 240/854), Ibrahim ibn Khalid al-Kalbi, founder of a school of *fiqh* in Baghdad.

Abu 'Ubayd: al-Qasim ibn Sallam al-Azdi al-Harawi: He devoted himself to hadith and *fiqh*. He was appointed *qadi* of Tarsus by Thabit ibn Nasr. He later went to Baghdad where he explained unusual hadiths and wrote books, and people listened to him. One of his books is *Kitab al-Amwal*. He went on hajj and died in Makka in 224/838-9.

Abu Ya'la: (d. 458/1065), Qadi Muhammad ibn Husayn al-Farrâ' al-Baghdadi al-Hanbali, a famous teacher. He wrote *al-Ahkam as-Sultaniyya* and *al-Mu'tamad bi usul ad-din.*

Abu Yusuf: Ya'qub b. Ibrahim b. Habib al-Ansari al-Baghdadi, born in Kufa in 113/731. He was the student of Abu Hanifa and the first to propagate his school, a hadith master and brilliant jurist with an extensive knowledge of *tafsir*. He acted as *qadi* in Baghdad for the khalifs, al-Mahdi, al-Hadi and Harun ar-Rashid, who made the Hanafi school the official state code for the Abbasids. He was also the first to write on principles (*usul*) of Hanafi *fiqh*, and was a *mujtahid*. He died in Baghdad in 182/798.

Abu'z-Zinad: (d. 131/748), 'Abdullah ibn Dhakwan, a Madinan *faqih.*

Ahmad (ibn Hanbal): (164/780-241/856), Imam of the *Ahl as-Sunna*, the founder of the Hanbali school and compiler of a *Musnad* which contains 30,000 hadiths.

'A'isha: (d. 58/678) the daughter of Abu Bakr as-Siddiq and favourite wife of the Prophet.

'Ali ibn Abi Talib: (d. 40/661) the cousin and son-in-law of the Prophet, having married his daughter Fatima. When 'Uthman was murdered in 35/656, he became khalif. He was assassinated by a Kharijite in Kufa.

'Amr ibn Hazm: one of the Ansar who died in 53/673.

'Amr ibn 'Ubayd: Abu 'Uthman, one of the earliest Mu'tazilites. He was originally a follower of al-Hasan al-Basri, but split with him. He was very friendly with al-Mansur. He died in 145/762.

Ashhab ibn 'Abdu'l-'Aziz al-'Amiri: He studied with al-Layth, Yahya ibn Ayyub, and Ibn Lahi'a. He kept Malik's company and learned his *fiqh* and was one of those who transmitted it. He had a collection called the *Mudawwana* of Ashhab, or the Books of Ashhab. He was a peer of Ibn al-Qasim but younger than him. Sahnun was the student of both of them. He was the leading *faqih* in Egypt. He was born in 140/757 and died in 204/820, a few days after ash-Shafi'i.

al-Awza'i: (d. 157/774), the principal Syrian *Shari'a* authority of his area and founder of a *madhhab*, which was later superseded by the Maliki school.

Ayyub as-Sakhtiyani: Imam Abu Bakr al-Basri the Follower and a leader of the *fuqaha'* and hadith scholars. Malik, ath-Thawri and others related from him. The Six Collections transmit from him. He died in 131/748 at the age of 63.

Bilal ibn al-Harith al-Muzani: (d. 60/680), a Companion.

al-Bukhari: Muhammad ibn Isma'il, (194/810- 256/870), the famous hadith scholar who produced the *Sahih*, considered to be the most reliable collection of hadiths.

Hammad ibn Salama: Abu Salama al-Basri, the *mufti* of Basra and a reliable narrator of hadith, excellent in Arabic and opposition to *bid'a*. He died in 167/784.

Hammad ibn Zayd: (d. 179/795), Abu Isma'il al-Azdi traditionist of Basra.

Harun ar-Rashid: the Abbasid khalif from 170/786 to 193/809.

al-Hasan al-Basri: Abu Sa'id ibn Abu'l-Hasan, one of the most important Followers in asceticism and knowledge. Born in Madina in 21/642, he met many Companions and transmitted many hadiths. His mother served Umm Salama, the wife of the Prophet. He died in Basra in 110/728 when he was 88.

al-Hasan ibn Ziyad al-Lu'lu'i: one of the famous students of Abu Hanifa and a *faqih* of Kufa. Wrote several practical works on law, including a handbook for *qadis*. He died in Kufa in 204/818.

Hisham ibn 'Abdu'l-Malik: Umayyad khalif, 105/724-125/743.

Hisham ibn 'Urwa: (d. 146/763), a Madinan *faqih*, son of 'Urwa ibn az-Zubayr.

Hudhayfa ibn al-Yaman: (d. 36/656/7), one of the earliest Muslims. He was governor of Ctesiphon under 'Umar. He related a large number of hadiths.

Ibn 'Abbas: 'Abdullah ibn 'Abbas, (d. 68/687/8), a cousin and close Companion of the Prophet. He is known as the greatest scholar of the first generation of the Muslims. He narrated many hadiths and is the founder of the science of *tafsir*.

Ibn Abi Du'ad: Abu 'Abdullah Ahmad ibn Abi Du'ad al-Iyadi, (159/776-252/865), the leading Mu'talizite and chief *qadi* under al-Mu'tasim and al-Wathiq. He was in charge of the Mihna. He was dismissed in 245/851.

Ibn Abi Layla: Muhammad ibn 'Abdu'r-Rahman al-Ansari (d. 83/765), a famous *faqih*. He had the rank of *mujtahid*.

Ibn 'Aqîl: in full Abu'l-Wafa` 'Ali Ibn 'Aqil ibn Muhammad ibn 'Aqil Al-Baghdadi Az-Zafari, (d. 513/1119), a Hanbali and Mu'tazili *mutakallim*.

Ibn Hibban: Muhammad ibn Hibban at-Tamimi al-Busti, a Shafi'i Imam and hadith scholar. He died in Bust in 354/965. He wrote *Kitab ath-Thiqat* and *Sahih ibn Hibban*.

Ibn Jurayj: (d. 150/767), a compiler of hadith.

Ibn Khuwayzimandad: Abu 'Abdullah Muhammad ibn Ahmad, a Maliki scholar who was a pupil of al-Abhari.

Ibn al-Majishun: 'Abdu'l-'Aziz ibn Abi Salama, (d. 164/780), a Madinan *faqih*. (There is also another scholar called Ibn al-Majishun, 'Abdu'l-Malik ibn Majishun)

Ibn Mas'ud: 'Abdullah ibn Mas'ud (d. 32-3/652-654), one of the earliest Companions, renowned for his knowledge, especially about the Qur'an and matters of *fiqh*.

Ibn al-Qasim: Abu 'Abdullah 'Abdu'r-Rahman. He was one of the companions of Malik who had tremendous influence in recording his school, since he was Sahnun's source for the the legal cases of Malik. He died in 191/806 at the age of 63.

Ibn Rahawayh: *see Ishaq ibn Ibrahim.*

Ibn 'Umar: 'Abdullah, (d. 73/693), a Companion of the Prophet, son of 'Umar ibn al-Khattab. He enjoyed universal respect because of his character and knowledge.

Ibn 'Uyayna: *see Sufyan ibn 'Uyayna.*

Ibn Wahb: Abu Muhammad 'Abdullah ibn Wahb al-Fihri al-Misri, one of the scholars in hadith. who stayed with Malik for about 20 years. He transmitted the *Muwatta'* and he died in 197/812 at the age of 72.

Ibraham an-Nakha'i: Abu 'Imran, one of the Followers and important *faqih* in Iraq. He was a *mujtahid* who had a *madhhab*. He died in 96/714.

'Ikrima ibn 'Abdullah: the client of Ibn 'Abbas, a Follower, one of the *fuqaha'* of Madina and its Followers. He is one of the Imams who is followed in *tafsir* and hadith. He died in 107/725.

'Imran ibn Husayn: a Companion who was later appointed *qadi* in Basra because of his knowledge of *fiqh*. He died in 52/672.

al-'Irbad ibn Sariyya as-Sulami: a famous Companion who was one of the *Ahl as-Suffa*. He is one of those about whom it was revealed, *"...neither against those who, when they came to you for you to mount them, and you said, 'I do not find anything on which to mount you,' turned away with their eyes overflowing with tears."* (9:92) He became Muslim early on and died in 75/694.

Ishaq ibn Ibrahim ibn Rahawayh: known as Ibn Rahawayh. He was known for his knowledge of hadith and revived the *Sunna* in the east. He compiled a four volume *Musnad*. He died in 238/853.

Isma'il ibn Ishaq al-Azdi al-Basri: (d. 282/896), the *qadi* and scholar in all areas of knowledge and in literature. He knew the book of Sibuwayh, the great grammarian, well and so was claimed to be one of the people of al-Mubarrad (another grammarian).

Jabir ibn 'Abdullah: al-Khazraji, (d. c. 74/693), a Companion. He related 1500 hadiths and taught in the Prophet's Mosque.

al-Ja'd ibn Dirham: the first to claim that the Qur'an was created. He was executed by Khalid ibn 'Abdullah al-Qasri.

al-Layth ibn Sa'd: al-Fihri al-Misri: (d.175/791), an excellent *faqih* about whom it was said, "He had more *fiqh* than Malik, but his companions wasted him."

Khalid b. 'Abdullah al-Qasri: governor of Iraq from 107/724 to 120/738.

Malik ibn Anas: (d. 179/795), the famous Imam of Madina in *fiqh* and hadith. One of the four Imams, founder of the Maliki school and author of the *Muwatta'*.

al-Mansur: Abu Ja'far, the Abbasid khalif, 136/754-158/775.

Muhammad ibn al-Hasan: *see ash-Shaybani.*

Muhammad ibn Ishaq: the client of 'Abdullah ibn Qays. He was concerned with knowledge of the *sunan* and studied a lot. He composed a famous *sira* of the Prophet. He died in Baghdad in 150/767.

Muhammad ibn Maslama al-Ansari: Abu 'Abdu'r-Rahman al-Madani, a Companion who was present at Badr. He was known as the "Knight of the Prophet" and died in Madina in 43/664.

Muhammad ibn Nasr al-Marwazi: Abu Zayd. (d. 371/ 981), a transmitter of the *Sahih* of al-Bukhari.

Muslim: Muslim ibn al-Hajjaj al-Qushayri an-Nishapuri, (204/820-261/875), a Shafi'i scholar and hadith master. His *Sahih* is said to be the soundest book of *hadith.*

al-Qasim ibn Muhammad ibn Abi Bakr: the nephew of 'A'isha and one of the seven *fuqaha'.* He was a *hadith* transmitter. He died in 108/725.

Rabi'a ar-Ra'y: (d. 136/753), Rabi'a ibn 'Abdu'r-Rahman, a famous *faqih* in Madina.

Rafi' b. Khadij: (d. 74/693), a Companion.

Sa'd ibn Abi Waqqas: (d. 55/675), one of the ten Companions promised the Garden and the last of them to die. He was a maternal uncle of the Prophet and became Muslim when he was 17, fought at Badr, and led the Muslims to victory at al-Qadisiyya. He was one of the six people of the Council after 'Umar's death.

Safina: the *mawla* of the Messenger of Allah. His name was Ruman and the Prophet named him Safina because, on one of his journeys, the Prophet saw him carrying his baggage and said, "You are a ship (*safina*)." Muslim and other authors of the *Sunan* transmit from him.

Sa'id ibn al-Musayyab: Imam of the Followers and their leader in knowledge. He had a grasp of both *fiqh* and hadith and was known for his worship and scrupulousness. He died in Madina in 94/713.

ash-Sha'bi: Abu Amr 'Amir ibn Sharahil, (d. 104 /721), a Follower famous for his intelligence, one of the reliable men of hadith in Kufa.

ash-Shafi'i: Muhammad ibn Idris, (150/767-204/820), the famous scholar and founder of one of the four *madhhabs.* He wrote *al-Umm* and *ar-Risala.* He was the first to formulate various legal principles, including that of abrogating and abrogated verses.

ash-Shaybani: Muhammad ibn Hasan, Abu 'Abdullah, born in Wasit in 131/748. A *mujtahid* Imam, he was educated by Abu Hanifa, Abu Yusuf and Malik. He wrote many books and died in Rayy in 189/804. His books include *Kitab al-Asl* or *al-Mabsut, al-Jami' as-Saghir* and *al-Jami' al-Kabir.*

Shurayh ibn al-Harith al-Kindi: (d. c. 78/692), of Persian origin, he came to Madina after the Prophet's death. He was judge in Kufa for 'Umar, 'Uthman, 'Ali and Mu'awiya.

Sufyan ath-Thawri: a scholar famous for asceticism and hadith. The Six Imams transmitted from him. He studied under 600 shaykhs. He died in 161/778 in Basra. He founded a school of *fiqh*.

Sufyan ibn 'Uyayna: (d. 198/813), one of the scholars and Imams from whom the compilers of the six *Sahih* collections all transmitted.

Talha ibn 'Ubaydullah: Abu Muhammad, the Companion, one of the ten promised the Garden and the first to unsheathe his sword in the cause of Islam. He was killed at the Battle of the Camel in 36/656.

at-Tirmidhi: 'Isa ibn Muhammad ibn 'Isa, (209/824 - 279/892), one of the great scholars. He was proficient in *fiqh* and had many books on the science of hadith. His book *as-Sahih* is one of the Six.

'Umar ibn 'Abdu'l-'Aziz: (d. 101/720), a Follower and a great Imam. People say he was the sixth of the Rightly- guided khalifs. He was khalif for two years and five months. His virtues are famous.

'Umar ibn al-Khattab: the *Amir al-Mu'minin*, (d. 23/643), one of the strongest defenders of Islam and greatest Companions. He became khalif after Abu Bakr and was murdered ten and a half years later.

Usayd ibn al-Hudayr: one the important Ansar who was present at both 'Aqabas, Badr and all the battles. He died in 20/640.

'Uthman ibn 'Affan: (d. 36/644), the third of the Rightly-Guided Khalifs and one of the ten promised the Garden. He completed the compilation of the Qur'an and many conquests were carried out in his time. He was murdered while reading the Qur'an in his house in Madina.

al-Walid ibn Muslim: Abu'l-'Abbas ad-Dimishqi: a *mawla* of the Umayyads and well-known scholar in Syria. He was born in 140/757 and died in 194/809.

Yahya ibn Sa'id: Abu Sa'id al-Ansari an-Najjari, originally of Makka. A *qadi* in Madina and then in Iraq. A major figure in the early science of hadith. He died in 143/760.

Yahya b. Yahya al-Masmudi: (d. 234/848 or 236/851), the pre-eminent jurist of Cordoba under 'Abdu'r-Rahman II. He met Malik and reconfirmed the text of his *Muwatta'* in the last year of Malik's life, i.e. in 179/795. He brought Maliki *fiqh* to Andalusia.

az-Zubayr ibn al-'Awwam: (d. 36/656), one of the most courageous of the Companions. He became Muslim when he was sixteen and was one of the ten promised the Garden, participating in Badr, Uhud and other battles. He was killed in the Battle of the Camel.

Zufar ibn al-Hudhayl: one of the more prominent pupils of Abu Hanifa. He died in Basra in 158/775 at the age of 48.

az-Zuhri: Abu 'Abdullah Muhammad ibn Muslim, (50/670 - 124/742), one of the earliest and most prolific collectors of traditions.

Index